1 MONTH OF
FREE
READING

at
www.ForgottenBooks.com

By purchasing this book you are eligible for one month membership to ForgottenBooks.com, giving you unlimited access to our entire collection of over 1,000,000 titles via our web site and mobile apps.

To claim your free month visit:
www.forgottenbooks.com/free544491

ISBN 978-0-483-61045-3
PIBN 10544491

A PROTESTANT MAGAZINE FOR ARMED FORCES PERSONNEL

VOL. 17 • DECEMBER 1959 • NO. 12

STORIES

ARTICLES

OTHER FEATURES

COVERS
   Front and Back: Our artist, James Talone, has pictured the lonely
      serviceman at the far corner of the world performing his duty,
      but nevertheless dreaming of home at Christmas.
   Inside Front: Christmas Fairs are held in every city and town through-
      out Germany. The most famous in Nürnberg, against the beauti-
      ful backdrop of the city's Gothic cathedral.
   Inside Back: Scenes like this one in Japan take place all over the world
      as GI's give gifts to foreign children. Here Sp3C Emmett K.
      Chappell brings Christmas cheer to Japanese girl at Salvation
      Army Girls' Home, Tokyo.
   ART WORK: Story illustrations by James Talone. Occasional spots by
      Volk.

Sound Off!

Thank You, Jim

Thanks tremendously for sending me copies of your beautiful September issue. You put out one of the top two or three most attractive religious journals.

James W. Carty, Jr.
Professor of Journalism,
Bethany College, W. Va.

An Editor Speaks

Seems to me LINK has a much more lively look lately, in art, layouts, etc. Congratulations!

Kenneth L. Wilson, Managing Editor
Christian Herald,
New York, N.Y.

Wants Nothing About Catholics

I am disappointed in your March, 1959 issue. Why do you have to write up Catholic Bob Crosby's family? This issue contributes almost nothing to Protestant information or solidarity. This is given not as a complaint but for your consideration.

A Friend
Postmarked in Philadelphia, Pa.

(continued on page 65)

STAFF

EXECUTIVE EDITOR: Marion J. Creeger; **EDITOR:** Lawrence P. Fitzgerald, **CIRCULATION MGR.:** Isabel R. Senar; **EDITORIAL ASST.:** Irene Murray

Subscription prices to civilians: $2.50 a year; $2.00 in lots of ten or more to one address.

For chaplains: Bulk orders to bases for distribution to personnel (in person, by mail, in back of chapel, etc.) invoiced quarterly at fifteen cents per copy.

Published monthly by **The General Commission on Chaplains** and Armed Forces Personnel at 201 Eighth Ave., South, Nashville 3, Tenn. Entered as second-class matter at the Post Office, Nashville, Tenn., under the Act of March 3, 1879.

Send notification of Change of Address and all other correspondence to Lawrence P. Fitzgerald, Editor, 122 Maryland Ave., NE, Washington 2, D.C.

All scripture quotations, unless otherwise designated, are from the Revised Standard Version of the Bible.

THE
THREE
STRANGERS

By PAUL McAFEE

THEY lay there during the long, cold December day, studying the Korean terrain before them. Sergeant Tom Williams was the recognized leader of the three. Corporal Bill Riley and Private Larry Crawford made up the remainder of the squad. They were cut off twenty miles from their lines in enemy territory, having been out on a scouting patrol when the enemy pushed their battalion down the valley, past the former perimeter. The others of their squad had been killed in a sharp skirmish with an enemy patrol twelve hours ago.

Williams pointed to a pass showing up between the high shoulders of two peaks. "That looks like the only way out. If we keep to the ridges we can reach it tonight. We'll need plenty of luck, but I think we can do it. Then we'll scout it out, and if it is clear, tomorrow night we'll go through."

"There was a bright star that came right up over the pass last night," said Crawford, his voice quiet. "I thought maybe we could guide on it tonight as we try to get there."

"It will be as good a guide as any," commented the sergeant. "You watch awhile," he gestured to Riley. "And keep your head down."

THEY moved up to the pass during the night, but were suddenly halted by a small house at the pass entrance. Again they lay through a long, chilling day, now particularly observing the house which lay between them and escape through the pass. Over the pass, now only fifteen miles away, lay their own lines. Night came finally, leaving a clear, starlit landscape about them. A dim light flickered from an opening in the house.

Williams, who had been watching the house, finally raised up slowly,

Three strangers twenty miles behind enemy lines at Christmas

turning to his companions. As he reached his full height, he could see the light again. It flickered as though someone had moved between it and a door or a window.

He squatted down and called them to him. "There's someone in the house, all right. We'll move on it. All the patrols are back of us now and we can be out of the pass by daybreak. Maybe there's some food in the house. At least we can get warm for awhile. They may report us in the morning, but by that time we will be gone."

Above them the pass loomed black, and again the star shone brilliantly over the entrance of the pass. "It's about midnight," whispered the sergeant. "Come on. Let's move in."

Williams stopped them when they were crouched back of the mud-and-stone surrounding wall. The low comb of the Korean house raised above them.

"I'll scout it out, you stay here," he ordered.

He left them and they huddled together. The cold penetrated to the bone. Riley could feel Crawford shivering and he himself was little less chilled. It seemed hours before they saw the bulky figure of Williams appear again.

"There's only a man and a woman," he said. "It looks like she has a new baby. And believe it or not—there's a goat and a cow in the room with them."

"Sure," whispered Crawford, "there's body heat from the animals. I wouldn't mind a nice, big shaggy dog to cuddle up to right now."

Moving up to the wall beside the door, they halted in the ink-black shadows of the roof's overhang.

Shortly Williams moved up quietly to the flimsy door. He hesitated momentarily, and then drawing back one weather-cracked boot, he slammed it against the door, and leaped into the room, Riley right behind him.

A skinny, thinly-bearded Korean man, awkward in his baggy pants, sprang to his feet and moved toward them, but was too frightened to say anything. The woman screamed weakly and then huddled back into her one thin blanket, her dark eyes enormous pools of fright. Under the blanket with her, only its wrinkled red face showing, was a newly born child.

Tense, angry, but fearful, the man backed slowly toward the mats. Now he spoke in his rapid tongue.

"He wants to know if we are Americans sent to kill them." Crawford's voice came from near the door.

"Do you speak this mess?" asked Williams.

"A little."

"Then tell him we ain't going to hurt them. Tell him we want some food, and we will warm for awhile. Then ask him directions through the pass."

Crawford spoke softly to the man who answered quickly.

Then Crawford said, "He says there is no food. We are welcome to warm ourselves. As to directions, the pass can be entered either by the main road or by a small trail that bypasses the main road and goes up along the slope of the mountain, above the road."

Sergeant Williams nodded and lowered his gun. "Okay. Crawford, you can come and get warm. Riley, see if there really is any food—he might be lying."

THERE was no food. To one side of the small room stood a skinny cow, and beside her an ancient goat, who eyed them casually as though he saw American soldiers every day. At the other side of the room was a tiny clay furnace, in which a small fire struggled to exist. Crawford approached and crouched over the fire, warming his chilled fingers.

"Sergeant . . . how much food do we have?" he asked, his eyes on the baby, his young face gentle.

"Four K-rations. Why?"

"Why don't we give them a couple? He says they haven't had food for three days. Barley soup is mighty thin eating for a woman that's just had a baby."

Williams grunted, his eyes brooding on the mother and child. "Yeah. I guess we can. We'll be back in our lines by noon. And if we ain't . . . two boxes of K-rations won't make much difference."

Riley spoke then, his bearded face

expressionless, his eyes hooded, veiling his thoughts. "We've got a blanket each and a poncho. Why not get rid of the blankets here? It will make easier traveling over the pass and the poncho will be all we need until we reach our outfit."

Sergeant Williams smiled crookedly, his rough, chapped face almost painful in the attempt. "You guys got anything else you want to unload on them before we go on?" He grunted. "A bunch of softies!"

Crawford gathered up the boxes of rations and the blankets the others handed him and held them out to the man.

The man did not touch them, so Crawford bent and laid them gently on the mats and stepped back. The man arose slowly, looking at them and then down at the gifts.

HE bent over and spread the blankets out and placed them over his wife and the baby. He held the two boxes of rations in his hands and looked from one of the soldiers to the other. Then he spoke softly. *"Ko mop sum neda,"* he murmured. His eyes softened and fear was gone from his features.

"He said thank you very much," whispered Crawford.

Williams stirred uneasily. One hand sought his pocket. "I just don't hold with giving too much stuff to these Koreans," he muttered. "You never know how much you can trust them." But his hand came out of the pocket holding a large square of red silk. "Here," he moved over and handed it to the woman. "I've had this ever since I was in Japan. I thought I'd give it to my girl back in Indianapolis. But . . . maybe the woman can use it for the baby." Riley grinned at Crawford, who smiled back and then they all three laughed and turned to watch the woman.

Her thin, claw-like hand reached out and took the red silk and hesitantly caressed it. Then she brought it gently to her brown cheek. Slow tears spread on her cheeks from beneath the closed lids. She opened her eyes then and looked at Williams, and smiled, and with the eternal woman-gesture, snuggled her cheek against the red silk square, her eyes expressing a benediction of thankfulness toward the sergeant.

Her husband bent over her, murmuring softly. She turned her gaze to him and then looked back at the soldiers, her smile embracing them all. One hand reached out and raised a fold of the warm army blanket and tucked it securely about the form of the child.

THEY left the hut an hour later and struck out toward the pass, the main road. A quarter of a mile along the road, a thin trail separated from it and wound up the mountain side. This was the rugged, high, bypass trail leading around the main road.

They paused momentarily at that point. the pass was now directly above them. The night sky was paling, the star had almost moved across the opening of the pass, seeking to hide its brilliance behind the bold face of the craggy peak.

"Say," muttered Riley to no one in particular as they stood there, "what day is this?"

Crawford answered, his thin face suddenly startled in the lightening gloom. "Why . . . it—it's Christmas! December twenty-fifth! Merry Christmas to you both!"

Neither answered. Williams moved his heavy shoulders impatiently under his pack and then grunted. "Come on . . . we've got ground to cover."

They moved off up the trail, disappearing in the covering brush and dips and crags of the Korean mountain slope.

■ ■

WORTH QUOTING: The girl who goes to pieces on the slightest provocation was probably never assembled properly in the first place. —J. C. Salak . . . Plastic surgeons can do almost anything with a nose except keep it out of other people's business.—Dan Bennett.

9

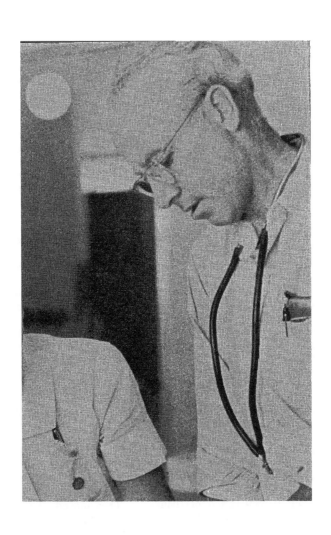

In the Footsteps of Albert Schweitzer

By Agnes Behling

"Only as every man strives for the happiness of others can he achieve happiness for himself"

WHEN his knowledge of foreign languages secured for Larry Mellon a place with the United States diplomatic corps during World War II, his family and friends breathed a sigh of relief. At last the young man seemed to have found his place in life!

But their hopes were short-lived, for soon he withdrew from the world of international politics and big business to "settle somewhere 'out West' to raise cows!" It was the same old story: Larry still was looking for something—still feeling that he was "not getting anywhere!"

As son of the co-founder of the Gulf Oil Corporation and the grand-nephew of the late Secretary of the Treasury, Andrew Mellon, with interests in the Aluminum Corporation of America, William Larimer Mellon, Jr., had been born to wealth. The Mellon mansion on Squirrel Hill in Pittsburgh was his home, that is, when the family was not spending the summer in the Canadian lodge or the winter along the Florida Keys.

He obtained his early education in private schools and from tutors. Later he dropped out of Princeton University at the end of his freshman year. Although his record had not been noteworthy, friends believed that he might have remained had he been required to work. As it was he went to work for the Mellon Bank and for Gulf Oil Corporation, but about the time he seemed to be making a name for himself in business, he surprised everyone by buying a cattle ranch in Arizona.

With misgivings his father became a co-partner, yet he knew his son could succeed once his interest was aroused. His gentle, modest mother, daughter of a religious, seafaring Scottish family, seemed to understand her non-conforming son and loved to visit his ranch home. When she died, Larry lost "the great spiritual force in his life."

His first marriage had been a

←◀◀ Dr. Larry Mellon, Miss Peterson, head nurse, and a young patient

11

Dr. Mellon and patient in "screening clinic"

failure. While divorce proceedings were pending, he met blue-eyed, auburn-haired Gwen Rawson, and later married her. She was at home on the ranch, and could do anything from work with the stock to survey the land. Four children were born to the Mellons, and their home life was a happy one.

THEN one evening Larry read a magazine article which changed the course of their lives. It was the life story of Albert Schweitzer of whom he occasionally had heard. It recalled his mother's answer to his childish question, "The best thing in life a man can be is a medical missionary." He had not understood it then; now the idea fascinated him. He bought and read several of

Schweitzer's works. There were similarities between the life of the famous missionary and his own. Like him, Schweitzer had found something missing in his life—a feeling that he had not found the right place. The humanitarian's life had been changed by a magazine article which portrayed the urgent need for doctors among the diseased natives of Africa. Albert Schweitzer began his medical studies at thirty, but he was more than forty before he built his hospital at Lambarene. Larry asked himself why he could not do the same.

When his ranch manager, a Frenchman, was due for a vacation, Larry disclosed his interest in the missionary of Lambarene, and suggested that the manager travel to his home by way of Africa. There he could visit Dr. Schweitzer and discover for himself if "any real good actually was being done." The manager undertook the mission and returned with convincing reports.

IN a letter to Albert Schweitzer, Larry explained his family responsibilities and his recognition of some of the difficulties involved, but closed with, "I want to do what you have done. What do you advise?"

The missionary in his nine-page reply did not minimize the obstacles ahead, not the least of which was the difficulty of older students to assimilate the required material. However, he radiated confidence, "The choice is difficult, and there are hardships, but you seem courageous. I urge you to pursue your new goal."

There *were* difficulties—many of them! Some were from relatives who felt Larry was turning his back on family enterprises. His concern for the underprivileged was interpreted as "a belated attack of adolescent idealism." Most disheartening was the stand taken by the medical colleges, but Larry Mellon's mind was made up and could not be changed. To counteract their opposition he offered, "Let me start. If I can't keep up with the other students, I'll quit on my own." His sincerity convinced Tulane University and he was accepted as a premedical student in 1948.

The family sold the ranches and moved to New Orleans where Gwen Mellon began her training as laboratory technician and surgical nurse.

The shy, slender man with the prematurely gray hair *did* seem out of place, and the work *was* hard. It was not unusual for him to memorize whole pages of material before examinations, only to discover that by the time he saw the questions he had forgotten much of the information. But he never lost sight of his goal: to build and equip a modern hospital in some underdeveloped area where its facilities and his medical skill was needed.

Larry arranged to meet Dr. Schweitzer on one of the doctor's few visits to the United States, and the two became close friends. Two years later the Mellons accepted an invitation to visit him at Lambarene, and there during his vacation, Larry learned through experience all that he needed to know about tropical diseases.

DURING his junior year Mellon took his family to Haiti on a trip which combined recreation with study. He and his wife gathered material for his thesis on the tropical ulcer so prevalent in the region. One of the trailer trips took the family to the Artibonite Valley, eighty-five miles northeast of Port-au-Prince.

The Valley was overpopulated in spite of its limited natural resources. There were too few medical students to cope with the widespread malaria, tuberculosis, venereal diseases, and yaws. Infant mortality was high due to inadequate obstetrical aid, and tetanus cases were common. Unemployment and poor housing, ignorance and apathy, adverse weather conditions and primitive methods of farming, as well as disease, contributed to malnutrition. Estimates state that in 1955 alone more than ten thousand died of starvation. The Mellons abandoned their search for a better place to build their hospital. This was the spot!

An agreement was made between the Haitian Congress and a non-profit organization, the Grant Foundation, for the financing of the project. As evidence of its gratitude, the government granted one hundred acres of land for the hospital site, an adequate supply of fresh water, the free use of buildings abandoned by the American Fruit Company, and exemption from duty on all imported building materials, hospital equipment, medical supplies, and food stuffs.

The building came into being very

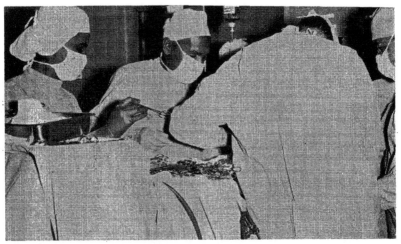

An operation being performed in the Albert Schweitzer Hospital at Chapelles

slowly, for there were numerous delays, but through them all, President Paul E. Magloire and Minister of Health Elie Villard gave their steadfast loyalty and support. Finally in December, 1954, Larry Mellon, now forty-six years old, stood on the Haitian hillside and watched the laying of the cornerstone of the new Albert Schweitzer Hospital.

By the following summer, Mellon had received his medical degree, served his internship, and completed a fellowship at the famous Ochsner Clinic. When the family came to the Artibonite Valley, the hospital was not completed, but they used the interval to acquaint themselves with the country, to gain the friendship and confidence of the people, and to "overcome their own shyness."

DR. Mellon urged Haitians to participate for he wished them to feel that the hospital was theirs. Day after day they worked in the hot sun, learning their skills on the

job, for only the foremen were experienced. Slowly the one-story, cyclone-earthquake proof building was finished, and its doors opened to patients in June, 1956. There were three air-conditioned operating rooms, X-ray facilities, a dental clinic, a pathological laboratory, all with equipment comparable with the finest hospital to be found in the United States. The fifty-five bed capacity could be expanded to seventy-five in an emergency, and plans called for a tuberculosis ward. The cost of about $1,500,000 was paid by Dr. Mellon who now assumed full charge.

About three-fourths of the natives who assisted in its construction live in the area served by the hospital, but others may be admitted by referral of their doctors. Water and outdoor cooking facilities on the grounds are provided for outpatients. The emergency entrance is adapted to "burro ambulances," often the only transportation available for the

14

poor natives whose annual cash income is less than $65. Dr. Mellon believes that patients do not want charity, therefore "a token charge" is made for medical services, "even if it is only one mango: anything will do if it gives people pride in themselves."

FOR the Mellons the hospital is "no rich man's toy." They are up by 5:30, and by 6:00 are at work. In addition to her duties in the hospital, the laboratory, and the office, Mrs. Mellon supervises the training of Haitian nurses' aids. Because Dr. Mellon hopes Haitians will some day take over so that he and his wife may go wherever they are needed, he trains the necessary native technicians, in addition to seeing several hundred clinic patients each week, making regular rounds, assisting in surgery, and consulting with staff members. Each day he makes frequent trips to the truck farm where he guides agricultural workers who apply their skills to raising better crops and more livestock on their own farms. When he is unable to go, his wife substitutes for him.

Privacy and leisure do not come until late at night when the visitors are gone, the letters are read or written, the case histories are completed, and the telephone is quiet. It is only then that the Mellons find time to relax, or that Larry may play some musical instrument for his own or Gwen's pleasure. Yet both agree that they never have known such happiness as here in their wonderful hospital.

Like Albert Schweitzer, Larry Mellon affirms, "If I had my life to live over again, I would do exactly as I have."

The waiting room at the hospital where patients wait with hope

Get Ready for Christmas

BACK in the heat of July, I happened to talk with a buyer for a department store. What was he thinking about? Christmas merchandise, no less! For merchants start to get ready for Christmas long before the first snow flies. In fact, they seem to keep pushing the Christmas shopping season further and further back toward the early days of fall.

Some of us would like to shout, "Whoa! Let's call a halt! Give us a breathing space between buying binges!" For "getting ready for Christmas" has come to mean for many persons in modern America a matter of buying presents, sending greeting cards, and eating more than usual. Christians know that there's much more to Christmas than can be seen in store windows.

Who's Coming?

About fifteen hundred years ago, the Christian church recognized that special preparation should be made

The Reverend Fred Cloud is Assistant Editor, Youth Publications, The Methodist Church, Nashville, Tenn.

for Christmas. So a special season, called Advent, was designated as a period of spiritual preparation for the receiving of Christ into the believers' lives. Advent, which might with justice be called "the New Year season of the Church Year," begins on the fourth Sunday before Christmas.

There's nothing new about an attitude of expectancy. The Hebrews of Old Testament times—especially the prophets—kept looking for great things from the hand of God. Isaiah wrote, centuries before Jesus,

For to us a child is born,
  to us a son is given;
and the government will be upon his
  shoulder,
  and his name will be called
"Wonderful Counselor, Mighty God,
  Everlasting Father, Prince of
  Peace." (Isa. 9:6.)

Christians saw in Jesus Christ the fulfillment of that prophecy. So, for them, Advent became a season of hope. It was a kind of annual rebirth of hope based on the reminder that God is with us.

By FRED CLOUD

Why Get Ready?

Christmas shopping takes time. So does the wrapping of presents, the addressing of cards, and the planning of Christmas parties. But when it comes to making spiritual preparation, one is inclined to ask, "Why get ready? Can't we just go to church on Christmas Eve and be done with it?"

Last minute shopping sometimes means that one has to accept leftovers, not usually what one would pick for a present if there were more time and a greater variety of things to choose from. Last minute spiritual preparation for Christmas nets the same result. This is not new, however; for on that very first Christmas Eve, Mary "gave birth to her first-born son and wrapped him in swaddling cloths, and laid him in a manger, because there was no place for them in the inn" (Luke 2:7). Many persons will have no place in their lives for Christ unless they make advance preparation.

We are persons who tend to focus on one thing at a time. If the glitter and tinsel of the customs that have grown up about Christmas are all that we give our attention to, we will miss the deeper meaning that Christmas holds. Here's a true story from December, 1958: Two women were looking at a manger scene in a downtown department store, and one said to the other in disgust, "Well, can you beat that? *Now* the churches are trying to take over Christmas!" Unbelievable? Ask six persons at random to tell you what Christmas means, in their own words.

How Can We Get Ready?

The birth of Jesus Christ takes on meaning because of the life that he lived as an adult, the way in which he met death on the cross, and his victory over death. So it's not enough to read the accounts of Jesus' birth from the Gospels (Matthew 1:18–2:12 and Luke 2:1-20). This season of Advent would be a wonderful time to read carefully one of the four Gospels in its entirety. Then, when Christmas arrives, you'll have a fresh understanding of what the Christian message is all about.

If you're familiar only with the King James Version of the Bible, this would be a good opportunity to get acquainted with a modern speech translation. Among the most readable are those by J. B. Phillips, James Moffatt, and Edgar J. Goodspeed. The Revised Standard Version retains much of the flavor of the King James Version, but it is based on more accurate scholarship than was possible in the seventeenth century.

What would Christmas be without carols? Music greatly enriches the whole experience of Christmas for millions of Americans. Personally, nothing helps me to get "the Christmas spirit" quicker than the singing of Christmas hymns and carols, and hearing them sung by church choirs, or on records. If we use our powers of selection some, we can cut back on the nonsense

17

Christmas music, such as "I saw mommy kissing Santa Claus" and "All I want for Christmas is my two front teeth," and emphasize the more beautiful hymns, folk carols, and songs with a Christian message.

Heaven forbid that anyone should interpret this to mean that Christmas is not a time for fun, however! Most chapels and churches stress fellowship activities—including Christmas parties—at this season. These too can help one to prepare for Christmas, for do we not sing, "Joy to the world"?

Pressure's on at this season to identify the Christmas "spirit" with "spirits"—the kind that come in a bottle. Four-color full-page ads in national magazines pour forth in profusion around Christmas, singing the praises of Old Scarecrow to chase your blues away. And the amount of drinking in the Christmas season in America has become a disgrace. No thinking person can imagine that this is the Christian way to get ready for Christmas, however.

God's Gift and Our Gifts

There's more than a little appropriateness to our custom of exchanging gifts at Christmastime. For, if we only reflect for a few minutes, we will realize that Christmas is a reminder that God gave his son to mankind to show us the way to eternal life.

Our gifts are seldom anything like as valuable, though they get more and more expensive. In fact, we noted ads a year or two ago for children's toy suits of armor at $100 up to $200. Some toys! One issue of *Life* magazine showed mink coats for dogs, more expensive than the clothes that many human beings wear. Our values get pretty scrambled, don't they, when we pay hundreds of dollars for a toy suit of armor while thousands of children in Europe and Asia starve for simple food? Christmas should send a signal so piercing as to cut through the materialistic fog that blinds so many persons today: the greatest thing you can give is your love, expressed in willingness to serve your fellow man.

Even today there is much hunger in the world. Both denominationally and interdenominationally, Christians can give to relieve hunger, and to clothe the cold. (One such channel is Church World Service.) Whether you're in America or abroad, you can share in this way and thus get ready for Christmas.

If you're stationed in Europe, Asia, or elsewhere abroad, you're in a good position to learn about Christmas customs of other cultures. After all, there's nothing sacred about a "white Christmas"! It's the event, not the trappings, that counts!

Visits in the homes of Christian families at the Christmas season—whether you're in America or abroad—is one of the surest ways of feeling the joy of the Christmas season. And joining in the worship of the congregations of Christians wherever you are will help you to be ready to receive the spirit of Christ into your life anew at the Christmas season, 1959. ■ ■

18

Christmas Quiz

By Vincent Edwards

ARE you a "Bible expert"? Can you tell the truth—when you see it? Well, here's a quiz that is especially designed to test your familiarity with the biblical story of Christmas. There are ten statements below, and all you have to do is to check whether they are true or false.

If you feel some need of "brushing up" on the Christmas narrative, read the first and second chapters of Matthew and Luke.

Each correct answer counts 10. Your final score may be graded as follows: 70—average; 80—good; 90—excellent.

Statement	True	False
1. The angel Gabriel appeared to Mary before the infant Jesus was born.		
2. After worshiping the Christ Child in Bethlehem, the Wise Men returned to Jerusalem to tell Herod where they had found Him.		
3. Joseph and Mary had to leave their home at Nazareth to go to Bethlehem to pay the tax decreed by Caesar.		
4. Jesus was the second cousin of John the Baptist.		
5. Three Wise Men traveled from the East to Jerusalem to seek the Christ Child.		
6. Because Herod plotted to kill the infant Jesus, Joseph was warned by God in a dream to flee into Egypt with Mary and the Child.		
7. The shepherds who worshiped the Christ Child in the manger at Bethlehem went away quietly without telling anyone about it.		
8. The chief priests and scribes were able to tell Herod in what city Christ would be born.		
9. Only one angel appeared to the shepherds on the hills of Bethlehem on the night that Jesus was born.		
10. After worshiping the Christ Child, the shepherds gave him presents of gold, frankincense and myrrh.		

(see page 30 for answers)

the search for intimacy:

THE FAMILY

BY GIBSON WINTER

THE most virulent poison created by industrial society is excessive loneliness. Our way of life uproots people, carrying them upward or downward in the struggle for success. Human bonds are pulverized. Those who cling to family ties are soon left behind in the economic struggle. Those who press forward find themselves cut off from friends and associates. We are the uprooted. We are the producers of things and the servants of machines. We live with things, ideas and prices. We rarely have time to live with people.

EVEN though the basic loneliness of our lives cannot be eliminated, we can share intimate contacts with others which make our loneliness creative rather than destructive. Our society has narrowed the sphere of intimacy almost exclusively to the immediate family of parents and children. The family is now the only antidote to the poisons of excessive loneliness.

The principal question about the American family is whether it alone can be a sufficient antidote to the poison of isolation. Can one intimate group meet all our needs for intimacy? Can the family meet such excessive demands for intimacy?

The strains in family life today can be attributed primarily to the narrowing of intimacy to the home. Two kinds of tension seem to be paramount in the modern home. The family is torn between its need for intimacy and its need for authority to guide its life. The family is also caught in a difficult struggle to provide children with a sense of belonging that does not tie them too closely to their parents. Both of these dilemmas have arisen as the family has become the exclusive sphere of intimacy on the American scene.

The more intense the loneliness of husband and wife, the more difficult it is to develop a center of authority in the home. Personal intimacy and authority are contraries which always exist in tension. The stronger the personal need for intimacy, the more disturbing is the subordination to authority. Since people today are suffering from in-

Condensed from *Love and Conflict: New Patterns in Family Life*. Copyright (C) 1958 by Gibson Winter. Published by Doubleday & Company, Inc. Used by Permission.

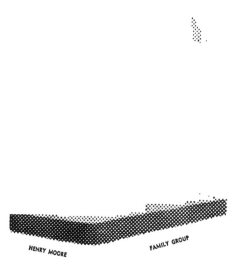

HENRY MOORE FAMILY GROUP

cern and support between equals. Two people stand together as equals in their concern for each other. No distinctions of ability, mental aptitude, riches or office can be allowed to dominate an intimate relationship. These barriers may exist in other settings, but they cannot be allowed to operate in friendship or marriage. Barriers of inequality are excluded from consideration in intimate relationships. Persons bound together by mutual love and concern exist for each other. Each will help the other and support the other. They counsel each other in difficulty and rescue each other in danger. These are the qualities of an intimate relationship. The intimate relationship assumes an equality as persons. However unequal the persons may be in ability, they are simply persons in their intimacy.

Authority, on the other hand, introduces inequality. Authority can only be exercised when one person subordinates himself to another on a particular matter. Let us picture the situation on the *Titanic* at the time of the tragic sinking. Husband and wife are on deck. The wife wants to stay with her husband. They have children at home. They resist the idea of being separated in this catastrophe. The husband insists that the wife enter the lifeboat and return to the children. In this crisis, the husband exercises an authority to which the wife subordinates herself. In this decision, they are not equal. So long as husband and wife agree, there is no issue of subordination and matters can be settled by consensus. When they disagree

tense needs for intimacy, we can assume that few families can tolerate much formal authority in the home. If the male authority is to be recovered in the modern family, it can be done very slowly. The central job of the family is to provide a sphere of intimacy in which excessive loneliness can be overcome. This is its primary task. All other concerns must be subordinated to the accomplishment of this task. If we accept this fact, we can handle the problem of authority without undue haste and without doctrinaire claims that it must be such and such. A proper division of authority can only arise as a fruit of personal intimacy.

THE conflict between authority and intimacy is clear from the nature of intimacy. An intimate relationship is a bond of mutual conon critical issues, authority introduces a problem of subordination and inequality.

It seems desirable that wives encourage their husbands to take a more authoritative role in the home. Their husbands have been forced out of the home situation by the circumstances of modern life. Such a recovery of male authority is bound to upset the equality of intimacy. It need not threaten the intimacy, if husband and wife feel assured of the mutual concern in their relationship. This suggests that the real issue to be worked through is the personal intimacy of the relationship. If the personal bond is soundly established, allowing room for privacy and a sense of support, then the division of authority may follow. On the other hand, many couples cannot deal with their personal intimacy because the power struggle has frustrated both of them. The modern family will undoubtedly lean toward equality and intimacy no matter how chaotic the home becomes. It is the nature of loneliness to demand its due at any cost. Nonetheless, full intimacy cannot develop in a chaotic home that is ruled by children. At the risk of disturbing equality and arousing conflict, the problem of authority will have to be faced for the long-range good of the family. There is no great danger of undue inequality if the biblical injunction is kept in mind and put into practice, "be subject one to another." This is the ground of equality on which intimacy rests. Husband and wife will differ in their abilities, interests, and respon-

sibilities. Despite these differences, they are joined as equals in the covenant of intimacy. Every inequality in marriage is subordinate to this fundamental equality. The two have become one flesh.

THE need for intimacy also creates tensions between parents and children. Such strains reflect additional problems of equality and inequality in intimate relationships. A fully intimate relationship is a person-to-person response between those who stand together in their personal life. At moments of deep intimacy, the persons shed the inqualities and differences. We occasionally experience such moments of intimacy across the barriers of inequality. A foreman and a worker may experience such personal encounter. These are moments when the responsibilities of our particular jobs are set aside and the fullness of our equality as persons takes the foreground. Then the work of life continues and we don our inequalities once again.

Parents treasure moments of full personal intimacy with their children. They cannot, however, fulfill their responsibilities to the children if they expect intimacy to be the normal state of affairs. Children are not equal to parents in the order of family life. If they were, the parents could not protect and guide them as they mature to full personal responsibility. Our deep needs for personal intimacy tempt us to transgress the inequality between parent and child. We want to draw children into more intimacy than is proper. We treat them as equals, when they need the protection of an unequal, parent-child relationship. Our own need for intimacy seduces us into excessive intimacy with children. The children cannot meet these excessive demands, so we reject the children.

Inequalities separate us in life, but they also protect us from unfair competition. No one expects a student to compete with his teacher on an examination. A child is exposed to emotional demands which he cannot meet when he is drawn into intimacy as an equal. A child is also forced to fulfill obligations as an adult, when he is treated as an equal. The transgression of the inequality of the parent-child relationship leads to excessive intimacy with children and makes them overly dependent. Ultimately it destroys their confidence in themselves. It also destroys their confidence in a protective and competent parent who can assure the stability of the world into which they are growing.

THE need for intimacy in our time makes it difficult for parents to walk this narrow line between personal intimacy with children and protective authority over them. It takes great skill to be a parent in our day, since the modern home carries the full burden of personal intimacy for our society. The capacity of parents to maintain this tension between personal intimacy and realistic discipline is the most important parental skill in modern family life. The remarkable fact about the modern home is the success with which so many parents are executing this difficult job.

THE much discussed rise in the rate of divorce over fifty years has largely come from the tendency to legalize most if not all marital arrangements. These figures are also augmented by the freedom for women to escape impossible marital situations. The family today is not much less stable than the family of a few generations ago. In view of

the strains in the intimate home, this suggests that more effort may be going into making a stable home than was necessary in earlier periods. Moreover, men are giving more time to their homes than was customary in earlier American or European life. Battle fatigue is suffered by so many women in the intimate home, but very few turn voluntarily from the intimacy of marriage to the business world. Children seem more rebellious today, although it is difficult to gain an adequate picture of child-rearing in earlier times. Delinquency rates certainly indicate an intensifying of rebellion among the young.

On the other hand, children are dependent on their parents until a much later age because of the increasing pressure for education. Such prolonged dependence is bound to generate strains. On the whole, the balance sheet for the intimate family looks reasonably good. The pressures of loneliness in our society have driven men and women to exert more time and effort on the intimacy of family life.

We seem to be entering an era of family living such as our society has not experienced. Family life is gaining rather than losing importance. This is, perhaps, an optimistic assessment of the situation but most of the evidence points in this direction. Life-long intimacy in marriage is one of the chief concerns of most young people. In *The Lonely Crowd*, to use David Riesman's phrase, men and women want time for intimacy.

There is little danger of casual marriages today, although most people seem concerned that young people enter marriage without serious thought. Of course, casual marriages do occur and are regrettable. Actually, however, our danger is that young people are trying too hard to succeed in marriage. They want so much to have an "ideal" marriage. Unfortunately, there is no such animal. Marriage is a give and take of love and conflict that never ends in an ideal state of harmony. Young people want successful marriages so much that the slightest difficulty becomes a major tragedy. Personal differences become a source of anxiety, whereas personal differences actually enrich an intimate relationship. Our modern search for intimacy leads us to identify sameness with intimacy. Thus, community becomes conformity and intimacy becomes intolerable.

THERE is no question that the intimate family can gain by extending its life through intimacies outside the home. No group can mature to its full stature in isolation. We may be expecting too much in imagining that the family can carry the full burden of intimacy for a whole society. This would suggest that the middle ground between family and commercial life needs to be strengthened. We need time for intimacy in friendship, neighborhood and church. We need some time for intimacy in every sphere of modern life. Whether such a transformation comes or not, we are now looking almost exclusively to the family for our deepest human needs. ■ ■

Letter from Home

By Minnie May Lewis

Dear Johnny:

Once we turned off the lights on a little boy's Christmas tree and rushed him to a hospital oxygen tent. There was little hope given for his recovery.

Christmas Eve came and went. The long vigil of the night broke into Christmas Day, the most agonizing day of our lives. That night your father's face was wet with tears and his young shoulders sagged as he walked down the long hospital corridor and trudged home to an empty house with its darkened gift-laden tree.

Solicitous nurses did all they could. I walked to the big window and gazed across heavily drifted snow to where Christmas trees bloomed in every window. I never felt so alone or helpless or empty. Where was God?

The sky was clear and studded with stars. One great star reminded me of Bethlehem's Star and the Child, whose birthday this was.

I began to pray. My faith proved greater than my sorrow. The emptiness faded. Suddenly I felt a very real and comforting Presence. I somehow knew that our son would recover.

Oxygen masks are familiar to that boy today as he climbs heaven's heights in a jet-propelled plane. Christmas tree lights play a lead role in his life again this Christmas Eve. We will be sharing his joy as he lights the lights on his own small son's first Christmas tree.

A blessed Christmas,
MOM

25

Story Behind
A
Christmas
Carol

By Chris Espy

NOBODY knows how many times Charles Dickens' *A Christmas Carol* (he always referred to it as *The Carol*) has been read to audiences large and small since it was written in 1843. But nearly everybody knows the story has become a classic, so much a part of our observance of Christmas that to many persons the season doesn't seem quite complete unless they read it, hear it read, listen to it on the radio or view it on television.

Dickens wrote it in less than a month because he was desperately in need of money. Then thirty-one years old, he not only had a wife and five children to support but a sister-in-law, brother and father who also lived in his home. He was deeply in debt and had already borrowed heavily both on his insurance policies and on books not yet written.

The story was practically a true one as he poured into it the yearnings, hurts, humor, joys and sorrows of his lifetime. Although his father, his sister Fannie, to whom he was devoted, and other persons less close to him had places in the book, most of the important characters were drawn from various aspects of his own personality. He was Bob Cratchit, for example, who could push aside all thought of debts and worries when one of his children became ill and throw all his love into caring for the young invalid.

He was Jacob Marley, Scrooge's business partner, aware that mankind and the common good of all was his business.

Through another facet of his make-up he was nephew Fred who delighted in parties, whether as guest or host, and who, although he laughed at his granite-hearted old uncle, could nevertheless become sentimental about him, especially at Christmas time.

As for the other side of the account, it must be admitted that Dickens was part Scrooge too. He was frequently indifferent to his obligations under a contract but would have nothing less than complete fulfillment of his own rights. He quarreled with his publishers over every cent of royalties and made life nearly intolerable for the artists who illustrated his works.

SCENES in *The Carol* were as faithful to life as its characters. After writing and rewriting in his rooms all day he often walked as much as fifteen or twenty miles at night through London's foggy streets seeking out precisely the right location for Scrooge's solitary rooms, the thoroughly gloomy building where he downed his lonely dinners, the proper site for the bakeshop and so on. As he wrote, even acted out the different parts before a mirror in his room so that he could observe his expressions and describe them accurately in the book. This habit undoubtedly helped him when, years later, he traveled widely giving his spectacularly successful public readings of *The Carol*. He had always longed to become an actor, and in the readings he cleverly mimicked the voices, expressions and mannerism of each character in the story.

Even that joyous bit in the book where the formerly dour Scrooge has at last taken Christmas to heart had its counterpart in reality. At almost exactly the same hour of the same day, although in a somewhat better part of London called Regent's Park, a window flew open as Dickens leaned out to greet the letter carrier and shortly discovered he hadn't missed Christmas either. The mail had brought him the glorious news that all six thousand copies of the first printing of *A Christmas Carol* had been sold on the first day and that a second and third edition were already being run.

THIS was the most welcome of Christmas presents to a hard-pressed family man. Dickens had already written *Pickwick Papers, Oliver Twist, Old Curiosity Shop, Nicholas Nickelby,* and *Barnaby Rudge* but now, although he didn't know it on that Christmas morning, he had written a masterpiece. Its success was especially gratifying to him because he had brought out the book on a commission basis, as a private venture. Furthermore, although a quality work he wished it to sell at a small price. He insisted on color plates and a fancy binding, yet the tag was only a modest five shillings.

The book, as the whole English speaking and many other parts of the world now knows, was, and still is, a tremendous success. It's one of those rare stories accepted by generation after generation of delighted readers of all ages, who reading or re-reading it at holiday time, say in the words of Tiny Tim, "God bless us every one."

■ ■

A Doctor
Writes a Book

By Bruce Hilton

HE was a doctor by profession, not a writer. He had a prison record and had long been suspected by the government of subversive activity.

And he was the author of what probably is the best biography of Christ ever written.

But the arguments against writing (including the fact that he was not a Jew and had never seen Jesus' native country) were far outweighed by the urgency Doctor Luke faced when he sat down to write the Gospel which bears his name.

Luke was worried by the smear campaign being stirred up in Rome toward his fellow Christians. Because they wouldn't worship Roman gods, words like "treason" and "subversion" were being used. Already it looked as though another round of jailings, torture and mass execution had begun for those who followed Christ's way.

The old doctor was worried, too, by a danger within the church. Many Christians still thought of the new faith as merely a revised, up-

Bruce Hilton is the editor of *Friends*, Otterbein Press, Dayton, Ohio.

to-date form of the Jewish religion. They wanted to limit participation to Jews—or to Gentiles who were willing to be circumcised and accept the Jewish ceremonial laws. They still thought of Christ as the long-awaited Messiah who had come to save Israel—and Israel alone.

By writing down all that was known about Christ's life and teachings, Luke hoped he could show the Romans that Christianity was not a movement designed to overthrow the government. And he hoped that his fellow Christians would see more clearly than ever before that Christ had died for everyone.

"Most Excellent Theophilus"

When he addressed his writings to "most excellent Theophilus," Luke apparently was approaching a VIP. The title, "most excellent," was used only for high officials in the Roman government.

The name itself was probably an alias; during the time the book was written the cruel Emperor Domitian was beginning a fifteen-year period of persecution of Christians unequalled even by Nero. For a government official to communicate openly with Christians could have been fatal.

One great student of the Bible, B. H. Streeter, thinks "Theophilus" was really Flavius Clemens, Domitian's cousin and direct heir!

We know that Flavius' wife was secretly a Christian, and that Flavius had shown interest in becoming one. We know too, sad to say, that Domitian later put Flavius to death for his pro-Christian leanings.

Whoever Theophilus was, we know he must have been honestly interested in the gospel. And how he must have thrilled to read it in a form which many have called "the most beautiful book ever written!"

"The Beloved Physician"

We don't know much more about Luke than we do about Theophilus. By reading between the lines, and from references like the one in Colossians 4:14 to "Luke, the beloved physician," we scrape together these ideas:

He was a Gentile—the only New Testament writer who was not a Jew. Probably he came from Antioch, a large city in Syria.

For years he had been a traveling companion of Paul, Mark, and other missionaries. He spent two years in jail with Paul in Caesarea, and had proved himself faithful even when others couldn't take it and quit.

He was an excellent writer and an especially careful historian. In his travels with Paul he must have met all the great leaders of the church, and pumped them for every bit of information about Jesus he could get. During the years in prison, he had time for research and study—and his book shows the results of all of this.

When he sat down to write he had a rich store of information. In addition to his notes, his memories, and a diary he had kept, it is apparent that he had the gospel books we know as "Matthew" and "Mark" available as references.

The Book Luke Wrote

"The Gospel of the Underdog," Luke's book has been called. More than any other gospel writer, the old physician was full of sympathy for the poor, the sick, the unwanted foreigners, the crooks and the bums of his day.

A man telling the life of Jesus couldn't put down everything, of course; there was too much to tell. So, inspired by God to a specific task, each writer seems to have chosen the sayings and actions of Jesus which best speak to that specific need.

Matthew wrote for Jewish readers and was concerned with proving that Jesus was the Messiah they had awaited; Mark set forth a simple, straightforward biography of Jesus, Son of Man; John wrote a theologian's book, deep with meaning.

Luke, concerned for the souls of his fellow Gentiles, emphasized the way Jesus seemed to ignore all social, racial, financial and political barriers when he said, "Come unto me. . . ."

29

As a result, Luke is probably the easiest book for us to read today. Writing for people like us, rather than for Jews steeped in religious tradition, he has a habit of giving Hebrew words a Greek explanation. He rarely quotes from the Old Testament. He begins dating his events from the reign of the Roman emperor, rather than the Jewish ruler. He never uses the Jewish term *rabbi* for Jesus; instead he has a Greek term meaning *master*.

The most important difference between Luke and the other three gospel writers, however, stands out when you see how certain minority groups are treated.

Luke seems to have gone out of his way to gather stories about Jesus' kindness to the hated Samaritans, for example. More than any of the other writers, he emphasizes the place of women—who in that day ranked down with slaves and Gentiles—in Jesus' life.

Luke is the only writer who tells us about Zaccheus, the crooked tax collector up in the tree. Or about the woman who bathed Jesus' feet with her hair in sorrow for her sins.

Or about the penitent thief on the cross.

Or about the prodigal son!

William Barclay, author of one of the best commentaries on Luke, points out that "It has been said that a minister sees men at their best; a lawyer sees men at their worst; and a doctor sees men as they are. Luke saw men and loved them all."

Through Luke we get a priceless picture of Jesus the Son of Man.

30

Luke's Profession

Luke's contact with illness and suffering seems to have been partly responsible for his deep compassion. And today, the practice of medicine still seems often to result not only in concern for suffering, but a special appreciation of God's part in relieving suffering.

There aren't many atheist doctors. And there are few people who haven't heard a doctor say, at one time or another, "I've done all I can; now it's up to God."

This reassuring faith can be just as strong a tool as the most miraculous wonder drug in a doctor's kit. Just as God guided the way of Doctor Luke as he showed us the compassionate Christ, He is today still guiding the hands of Luke's successors—who express that same compassion with pillbox and scalpel.

■■

If at first you do suceed, it's too easy; try something else.—V. M. Kelly

ANSWERS TO
"Christmas Quiz"
(*see page 19*)

1. True. (Luke 1:26-28)
2. False. (Matthew 2:12)
3. True. (Luke 2:1-5)
4. True. (Luke 1:36)
5. False. The number is not stated. (Matthew 2:1)
6. True. (Matthew 2:13)
7. False. (Luke 2:17)
8. True (Matthew 2:4-6)
9. False. (Luke 2:13)
10. False. The Wise Men gave these gifts. (Luke 2:16-20; Matthew 2:11)

"Something for the Boys"

The United Voluntary Services Stamp Lady—Mrs. W. Lansing Rothschild—visits with members of her stamp club at Ft. Miley V.A. Hospital, San Francisco. Left to Right: Thomas, Warner, Atlee, and Le Clair.

ONCE a week, without fail, hundreds of hospitalized veterans in many states look forward at mail time to a familiar red, white and blue envelope from the UVS Stamp Lady.

Each envelope contains from five hundred to one thousand colorful postage stamps, carefully packaged in waxed paper and ready to be proudly displayed in stamp albums.

Collecting these stamps from many sources, and preparing thirty thousand of them a week for mailing, has become a full time, year-round volunteer job for Mrs. W. Lansing Rothschild, the Stamp Lady.

"I didn't know one stamp from another when I began this work ten years ago," confesses Mrs. Rothschild, whose husband is president of the Yellow Cab Company in San Francisco.

Nevertheless, this personable grandmother, who was a volunteer during World War II, was determined to do "something for the boys" convalescing in V.A. hospitals.

She started the Stamp Club program on the suggestion of a friend and has been at it, without letup, ever since.

To gather stamps for the program, Mrs. Rothschild enlists the help of banks, import houses, travel agencies and individuals.

31

Mrs. Rothschild removes stamps from the envelopes or scraps of paper to which they are glued by dumping them, by the thousands, into a dishpan full of cold water, containing a small amount of salt to fix the color.

She lays the stamps out to dry on a desk blotter before packaging them in protective wax paper envelopes.

Mrs. Rothschild then mails her weekly gift of stamps to patients in more than twenty veterans hospitals where she directs UVS Stamp Clubs by remote control. Each patient wishing to start a stamp collection is mailed a kit containing an album, hinges, tongs, a magnifying glass and an initial selection of stamps.

With his weekly issue of stamps, he sometimes receives a personal letter from the Stamp Lady, and on holidays, the stamps are invariably accompanied by a cheery greeting card.

Mrs. Rothschild is rewarded many times over for these thoughtful gestures. A Mother's Day never passes but what she receives dozens of cards from boys she has never seen, and she treasures the hundreds of heartfelt notes of thanks sent her over the years by the Stamp Club members. Typical is this example from a veteran patient in a tubercular hospital:

"Dear Mrs. Rothschild: Thank you so much for the Valentine and the stamps. It helps a lot to know that nice people on the outside think of you."

Besides directing UVS Stamp Club activities by mail, Mrs. Roths-

"My baby!"

child pays frequent visits to San Francisco Bay Area veterans hospitals, where she distributes stamps in person. She calls at Fort Miley Veterans Hospital in San Francisco regularly each Wednesday afternoon, and every other Tuesday night she goes to Letterman Army Hospital.

Once a year, Mrs. Rothschild rents space in a downtown hotel and stages a public stamp exhibit.

"There is no beginning and no end to this program," says the Stamp Lady. "The only problem—and it's a continuing one—is in getting enough stamps to supply all the boys who would like to collect them."

Mrs. Helen F. Lengfeld, national president of the United Voluntary Services, urges persons to send stamps to Mrs. W. Lansing Rothschild, UVS National Stamp Club Director, 1990 Eighth Avenue, San Francisco 22, California. ■ ■

RETROSPECTION

H AD I by chance been staying
    In Bethlehem that night,
And known of Mary laying
Her babe by lantern light
Within a cattle shed,
You would have heard me saying,
"Here, take my room instead!'

A H, yes, it is so thrilling
    To think on bygone things—
To see His presence filling
With lustre like a king's
A room-that-might-have-been—
And yet be all unwilling
Today to take Him in.

—GEORGE L. KRESS

A LAYMAN'S CHRISTMAS PRAYER

O UR Heavenly Father . . .
    Fill our hearts with true courage, so that we will have no room for
cowardice.

Fill our spirits with Christ-like humility, so that we will have no room for
selfish pride.

Fill our souls with genuine forgiveness, so that we will have no room for
hate.

Fill our minds with keen understanding, so that we will have no room for
prejudice.

Fill our lives with eternal gratitude, so that we will have no room for self-
pity.

Fill our consciences with Christian compassion, so that we will have no room
for unconcern.

We pray in the name of the Prince of Peace.
Amen.

—WILLIAM A. WARD

33

Joyful
and
Triumphant

By Robert A. Elfers

WHEN the public address system began to play "It Came Upon a Midnight Clear" for the third time, Joe opened his eyes and stared up at the ceiling that arched high above the benches in the vast waiting room.

"Oh! You're awake!"

For a moment, he did not realize that the girl was speaking to him. Then, when he looked at her, he was so astonished by her loveliness that he answered rather brusquely, "I wasn't asleep."

"And you can talk, too!" She struck gloved hands together and the cluster of gold trinkets on one wrist tinkled. "How wonderful!"

Very carefully, he studied her. Her face was framed in a tight black hat from which flowed waves of richly glinting brown hair. Her eyes were large and violet gray. A slender, graceful nose. Smooth and curving lips. She sat erect and

"I hate Christmas," Marie said, "because love is a lie. Love doesn't exist." Did Joe convince Marie that she was wrong?

poised, a slender figure in carefully tailored black suit and black pumps with stiletto heels.

He shook his head. "No," he said, "I've never met you. I'd remember if I had."

Her laughter rang like sleigh bells. "I came to wish you Merry Christmas. I thought I'd cheer you up."

"Is that what you usually do on Christmas Eve? Come to Union Station and just go up to anybody at all and start talking to them?" He grinned. "Not that there's anything wrong with it, but after all, a girl like you. . . ."

She sat a little straighter and interrupted him. "You're not anybody, are you? You're in the Army. I always thought soldiers who were away from home on Christmas Eve were lonely."

Joe looked away from her. Most of the benches around them were empty, the whisperings and shufflings of travelers were subsiding, a man who was apparently the owner was locking up the station's drug store and hanging a sign that read "Season's Greetings" on his door.

"Do you know much about soldiers?" he asked.

"Sure," she answered, raising her chin in tempting arrogance. Then she stood up. "Come on, let's go."

He rose slowly because she was standing. He did not pick up his overcoat. "Where do you want to go?" He was faintly suspicious of her actions.

"Anywhere. A restaurant. Walking. Or anywhere. You don't want to spend Christmas Eve in a railroad station, do you?" She hesitated, and it was as if a shadow had touched her face. "Or is your train leaving soon? Maybe you don't have time."

"No. I have time."

"Well, then—" Surprisingly, her voice broke. "Well, then, let's go."

"What's your name?"

"Marie."

"Marie, I don't think I will." He felt awkward, looking down at her and saying the blunt words.

She stood motionless, as if even her heart had stopped beating. Then a tremor moved through her body. The life color in her cheeks faded and her lower lip began to tremble. A glistening grew in her eyes but before the tears could fall, she turned her head and hurried away.

JOE watched her until she went through a doorway and out of sight. Then he sat down again, his long legs sprawled in front of him and his big hands open on the seat beside him. He raised a hand and raked it through his short blond hair. The tenseness of traveling—the long miles, the bus breakdown, the missed train—were pulling at him. He felt suddenly very tired and depressed. He would not let himself look at the great clock hanging from the ceiling, for he knew that he still had hours to wait be-

35

fore he boarded the train. And then he would ride through the darkness of Christmas Eve until the sky lightened. The train would stop at the village and he would walk the wrinkled, wind-swept streets to the small house where two old people— his aunt and his uncle—would embrace him, trying to act as parents for a young man they scarcely knew. He would respond as he should, out of respect and family duty and knowledge that there would not be many more years that he could spend Christmas with relatives.

The memory of the girl—young and beautiful and appealing—engulfed his thoughts. He wondered what had seemed unreal about her, what warning he had sensed in the enjoyment of her company. *I'm a fool,* he thought savagely. But deeper than the thought he knew another voice that said, *Not so, my friend, not by what you intend yourself to be.*

Wearied of his torment, his loneliness, the mockery of Christmas carols sung by a metal horn and echoed by granite walls, he stood up. Perhaps the coldness of the night would numb him to his feelings. He put on his cap and was reaching for his coat when someone spoke behind him.

"I suppose it won't do any good, but I want to say something to you."

He turned and saw the girl. Her face was pale, except for the rosy darkness painted by tears around her eyes. But the eyes themselves were now jewel-hard and blue as polar ice, and her voice made hailstones of her words.

"I want you to know that I wasn't trying to proposition you or anything like that. I lied to you about talking to you because you were lonely. I just wanted somebody to talk to myself. I hate Christmas . . . but never mind about that. I just wanted somebody to talk to and that's all, you big oaf. My luck was bad: I picked on you."

By the time he had recovered from the lashing, she was far across the waiting room. She had a fur coat around her shoulders now and thrust her arms into it without breaking stride.

"Wait a minute," he said foolishly, and started after her. When he saw her go through an outer door, he began to run.

He was unprepared for the cold outside. A cruel wind struck him in the face as he turned the corner and he staggered for a moment. He thought he saw a small figure ahead under the lamplight. Following, he found himself on a bridge swept bare of snow by the wind gusts.

He was sure he saw her when he was across the river. She seemed to be running. He decided to circle a block and meet her from the other direction.

But the block was longer than he thought, and when he was back on the street where he had seen her, she was no longer in sight.

FOR a while he wandered aimlessly in the city's empty streets, accompanied only by his blurred reflection in great, dark department store windows. He hoped he might find her, but if he had, he was not sure what he would say. He might apologize, although he wasn't sure for what. He might ask her what she had against Christmas. He might say simply that he was lonely, too.

He gave up the search finally and was looking for a bus that would take him back to the station when he came upon a church where a Christmas Eve service was being conducted. A sign read, "Everyone Welcome."

He could imagine the interior of the church, warm lights on brown woodwork and green deckings of holly and pine, the pews filled with family groups, the air stirring with organ peals, the atmosphere rich with expectancy and joy and friendliness.

Yet, as a stranger, he was about to turn away when a man and woman, going in, smiled in a friendly way as they passed him. So he followed them up the steps and inside.

He found a seat in the last row, and as he sat down, the pastor began to read the Scripture lesson. It was the second chapter of Luke, the story of Bethlehem's immortal night. Joe listened to the reading and forgot his self-consciousness. He closed his eyes and the words seemed to come from a great distance. They swept him up gently and he heard his father speaking them to him above the Congo's rush, saw his mother in her chair reading by the light of the Christmas tree in Oregon; remembered the service at college when his roommate's soft Southern voice rolled the words deeply through the chapel.

And as he remembered, he realized that while the voices of the past were silent, the words were still heard, that new voices were speaking them, that new voices would always speak them. He understood, with all his capacity for understanding, that the words would never be lost, that they would live forever and that what they spoke of God's gift of love would forever be true, and would forever be spoken to lonely travelers in the night.

The service moved its stately, joyous way and Joe prayed with the people about him, sang with them, listened with them to the pastor, all the time with the great light of his discovery fierce and radiant within him.

WHEN the benediction had been said, he stood up, shook hands and exchanged greetings with a man next to him and a red-cheeked old lady in front of him. He was about to go into the vestibule when he looked back at the crowd in the sanctuary and saw the girl. She was by herself, seeming to stay apart from the clusters of people near her, a strained smile coming to her lips when someone spoke to her.

He made his way slowly toward her and she didn't see him until he was only a few feet away.

"Hello," he said awkwardly, aware of the onslaught of her eyes. "Do you mind if I speak to you?"

She turned away and joined the stream of people going down the aisle. Joe followed her slowly. He was wondering what to do when he became aware that the red-cheeked old lady who had greeted him so heartily was now talking to the girl. Somehow, Joe was pulled into an exchange of pleasantries that became a complex question and answer session. With a variety of "tuts-tuts," expressions of anxiety for young people away from home, and cheery motherings, the old lady led them implacably out of the church and into a rumbling red station wagon driven by a muffled, merry-eyed old man named George. George ground the gears twice and the car shot forward, heading toward the railroad station. In a surprisingly short time, the girl and Joe walked through the station door, waved at their benefactors, and watched the station wagon drive off.

There was a period of silence and Joe began, "Well, if you—"

"I need a cup of coffee," the girl said.

He looked around the waiting room. It was still brightly lighted, but almost empty of movement. The great clock's hands pointed to 12:30. "Everything's closed," he said. He stared at the clock. "It's Christmas."

She looked up at him and this time he saw not anger in her eyes but only emptiness.

They sat on a bench, she huddling to herself within her fur coat, he upright and uncertain.

"I wish very much," he said slowly, without looking at her, "that somehow we had made friends. This is not a good time to be without friends."

She was silent, and after a moment, he went on, "If you would rather, I won't talk. I'll even go. My train leaves in twenty minutes."

The words disappeared into the vast emptiness around them. He waited for a while, then stood up and looked down at her. He intended to say merely "Goodby" and leave. But when he saw her from above, her smallness, her aloneness, her weariness—when he remembered the lostness in her eyes—he knew he could not say it.

AS if she sensed the emotions struggling within him, she looked up and studied his face. "Come," she said, "sit down again."

She watched him as he came next to her. "I was right about you after all," she said. "I knew what kind of a man you are. That's why I spoke to you in the first place. I'd never done that to anyone before. I was horrified when you turned me down. And angry, because you seemed to think I was a tramp."

"No," he protested. "I didn't think that. At least. . . ."

"It doesn't matter. I'm sorry that I've ruined your Christmas Eve. You couldn't even escape me in church."

The memory of his discovery flared within him. "I was lonely when I went in," he said. "But something happened. You know, I'm the son of missionaries. If you knew me, you'd know I'm a pretty religious guy. So you'd expect me to get something out of church. I did this time anyway."

She listened to him intently, and he was trying to command the words that would explain what he meant when she said, "Are you on your way to visit your parents now?"

He shook his head. "They're both dead. I'm going to spend Christmas with some relatives."

"I'm going home to my parents," she said. "Coming home from college to spend the holidays with my parents." There was a thread of mockery in her voice. "Coming home. I think sometimes that my mother and father hate each other. Have you ever spent Christmas in a home where there's no love?"

He saw the pain in her face and her fingers clenching. "No. Never."

"I hate Christmas," she said.

"Even if they don't love each other, I'm sure they must love you."

She looked at him squarely, her loveliness in repose. "Love is a lie," she said. "Love doesn't exist."

For some reason, over the public address system, there came again suddenly a Christmas carol—just a few bars—and then the magnified popping of a switch and a nasal voice roaring out: "The 12:50 to Philadelphia. Track 7. All aboard!"

Joe stared at the girl. "That's my train. I've got to go. Marie, you're wrong." He spoke with the glory of the Christmas story burning clear within him.

"That's what Christmas is all about. God so loved the world that he gave his son. You and I—maybe we're alone. But we're not—not really. God is with us just as he was there in Bethlehem that first Christmas. Because he loves us. He loves *you*. He does. He loves *you!*"

He thought he saw a response in her eyes but then she dropped her head. When she looked at him again, he was sure that he had failed.

He did not trust his voice to say goodby. He hurried toward the train and, reaching the doorway, turned to look. He waved at her distant figure but was afraid she did not see him, but then she did answer, with a quick, reaching gesture. ■■

Why My Mother Disliked Christmas

By Arnold Porter

MY mother took a dislike to Christmas one year for two reasons: First, my two-year-old sister hit my mother over the head with my Christmas hammer; and my grandfather tied my sled behind his car with me on it and dragged me into a deep irrigation ditch.

These incidents were not deliberate attempts to discourage my mother but they were remarkably successful for all their lack of purpose.

My sister now says (although I prefer to think she doesn't remember a thing) that she just didn't know what to do with a hammer. Grandfather's explanation admitted my wisdom in sliding in the snow beside the road, but emphasized my stupidity in not getting on the road to cross the culvert.

Pagan Aspects of Christmas

My mother's many dissatisfactions with Christmas reached their high point that year. She was never fond

Chaplain (Captain) Arnold Porter is with the 48th Air Base Group, APO 119, New York, N.Y.

40

of Christmas but through the years her Christmas spirit gradually improved. Here are some of the reasons mother wanted us to pass hurriedly on our Christmas way.

The commercial aspect of the season bothered her. She thought it was pagan and she was right.

Late December was a pagan holiday long before Christ. The Romans celebrated Saturnalia at that season with green boughs, flowers and gifts of candles and cakes. The Druids used mistletoe for sacred decoration then. Holly and ivy were cut by the Saxons at the same season for their religious celebrations. In Scandinavia and other countries the winter solstice, the shortest day in the year, brought the people to the hilltops with bonfires. Candles and torches were also used to help the faltering sun revive.

All of this was inherited by the church deliberately but with an earnest and not completely successful attempt to change the significance. Pope Gregory in 601 instructed his missionaries:

"Let the shrines of idols by no

means be destroyed but let the idols which are in them be destroyed so that the people, not seeing their temples destroyed may displace error and recognize and adore the true God. And because they were wont to sacrifice oxen to devils some celebration should be given in exchange for this. They should celebrate a religious feast and worship God by their feasting so that still keeping outward pleasures they may more readily receive spiritual joys."

When the "outward pleasures" ignore the "spiritual joys" the ancient pagan trappings and the modern commercial paganism are combined into an empty secular holiday.

The Real Meaning of Christmas

"What was the day when Christ was born?" my mother wanted to know. And of course no one knows the real date or day. "Well," she finally said, "it doesn't matter." God was born as a man and we celebrate the fact, not the date. Like the birthdays of the kings and queens of England, which are always celebrated in the summer because of the garden party weather, the birthday of our Lord is admittedly inaccurate.

Today for instance could be Christmas. In fact every day is Christmas for the Christian, for God's reconciling love expressed through Christ is real every new day of the year.

"Christmas is for children," my mother said. But she told us its true meaning was eternal, mature and world-wide. While Santa Claus is supposed to visit around the world in his various costumes and names, Christ actually brings the love of God to all mankind.

Even communist Russia included Christmas trees in its exhibition of Russian culture in New York last July. "Everyone has Christmas trees," the communists said. Well, Christmas really means that Christ is looking for room in the human heart and wants to make that heart his dwelling place. Christmas is love. God loves us and desires that we live in peace and love toward one another. Obviously this is a year-round opportunity for everyone.

"I can't stand all that sentiment," my mother said. It is useless and shouldn't be "stood." Naturally, "everybody loves a baby." But as parents know, infants at 0130, hungry, wet and screaming, demand responsible action as well as sentiment.

Christ did not remain an infant. He grew up and his demands on his followers are enormous. It is easier to be overcome with sentiment at Christmas than it is to fulfill mature Christian responsibility throughout the year.

Well, my mother worked her way through the Christmas problem for herself and her family but so far she hasn't given any of her grandchildren either a tool chest or a sled. ■▀■

Christmas says to us that the greatest fact about our world is that God is in it; God with his offer of power and life.—*Presbyterian Record*

41

Christmas
in
the Bavarian
Tyrol

By Rip Lynnfield

←■

**Train on Zugspitz railroad climbs
slowly through Bavarian mountains**

THE tannenbaum stood illumi-
nated in the village square
surrounded by gaily painted, Hansel-
and-Gretel-like cottages. Townspeo-
ple dressed in lederhozen and green
Tyrolean hats greeted me jovially
as they bustled by: "Weihnachten"
... "Weihnachten."

"Merry Christmas to you, too,"
I replied cheerfully in English.

But it was the tannenbaum—"the
Christmas tree for everyone"—which
held my attention. To a lonely serviceman four thousand miles away
from home, it, too, seemed to
whisper "Weihnachten."

This was my Christmas holiday
not so long ago, while serving a tour
of duty in Germany with the U.S.
Air Force. To the fortunate service-

man stationed in Europe today, I
can say from experience that a
Christmas leave spent in Bavaria
will prove a rare and unforgettable
experience.

Each December the USAREUR
Leave and Rest Center in Garmisch,
Germany, is visited by hundreds of
American military personnel on
leave from their bases around Europe. Unfortunately, however, due
to the fact that most of the billets,
hotels and recreation centers are located there, many servicemen seldom
take the trouble to leave Garmisch
to explore the many out-of-the-way
villages just around the corner from
the leave center.

They don't know what they are
missing. For in many ways these

42

same obscure little villages supply the rare experiences that a man can look back on long afterward.

TAKE Oberammergau, for example. This peaceful little village, nestled among towering Alpine mountain ranges, has been closely allied to the life of Christ for hundreds of years.

No doubt you have heard of Oberammergau in connection with the decennial presentation of its famous Passion Play, traditionally produced every ten years. Almost every man, woman, and child in the village—a cast of over twelve hundred persons—takes part in the play which next will be given in 1960.

But Oberammergau is famous for other reasons. While I was there on leave, I visited the local museum with its collection of wood carving exhibits. In homes scattered around the globe this Christmas, families will place a small Christmas crib at the foot of their tree to celebrate the holiday season. The carving of these cribs and nativity scenes is the chief industry of Oberammergau's woodcarvers.

The custom of decorating Christmas trees with nativity scenes was originated by the Germans. In this way they identified the tree with eternal life.

Oberammergau, sleepy little German village among the towering Alps of Bavarian Tyrol, is site of world famous Passion Play. To be given in 1960

ANOTHER treat that awaits the visitor to Oberammergau is the old Christmas Manger, located at 5 Daisenbergerstrasse. Here you will view a vast collection of puppets and dolls dressed in the costumes of the characters appearing in the Passion Play. Some of these costumes are over a hundred and fifty years old.

A final sightseeing must is the Village Church of Oberammergau, built between 1736 and 1742, with its beautiful paintings by Franz Zwink, an artist of the late 1700s. Zwink also painted the many gay frescoes decorating the house fronts that you see around Oberammergau which lend the village its cheery atmosphere.

FROM Oberammergau, Berchtesgaden is just a few miles away. If you are in this German village on the night before Christmas, you probably won't encounter too many Germans in the street. The reason is that Christmas Eve in Germany is a highly solemn and religious occasion. Most Bavarians will be attending midnight services and exchanging gifts upon their return home from church.

Just over the Alps from Berchtesgaden is the Austrian city of Salzburg. Near here, on a Christmas Eve in 1818, starving mice ate the bellows of the village organ and played an indirect part in the creation of the beautiful Christmas carol, "Silent Night, Holy Night." Salzburg also is the birthplace of Mozart and you will be able to view his own handwritten compositions there in-

Olympic Ice Stadium at Garmisch

cluding the violin he once fingered with his genius.

Near Garmisch is another little village, Mittenwald, whose busy craftsmen made the town world-famous for its beautiful violins. A trip to Mittenwald will take you back into the Middle Ages when the merchants of Venice made the town a bustling music center from 1487 to 1693.

FINALLY, the serviceman has Garmisch-Partenkirchen itself as a winter playground. In the center of the town stands the huge Olympic Stadium—scene of exciting ice shows and sporting events. High in the surrounding mountain range are the Zugspitz—Germany's highest mountain—where skiing, bobsledding, and hiking may be enjoyed. For even in winter, most Tyrolean footpaths are kept free from snow, making sightseeing convenient for anyone.

If you are lucky enough to be invited into a German home for

44

Christmas—which is usually a private occasion reserved for one's immediate family—you will discover that it is celebrated not so very different from your own Christmas.

Presents will be placed under the tree or on a table. The family will gather together to sing the favorite old German Christmas carols.

There is one distinct difference, however, from an American Christmas. After the singing, a bell is rung. This signals the departure of the Christ Child who has left gifts for the family.

This is but one of several Christmas customs celebrated in Bavaria during the holiday season. There are many, many more. Some you may be fortunate enough to see in person or, knowing of them, will be able to watch for them; others you may never witness.

One custom that particularly delights American servicemen are Berchtesgaden's famed Christmas Shooters.

There are roughly five hundred members of this famous organization. One week before Christmas, at exactly 3:00 P.M. church bells are rung and members fire their large pistols to hail Christ's birth. The grand finale occurs on Christmas Eve, when all five hundred members fire their pistols in unison.

ANOTHER beautiful custom in Berchtesgaden also occurs on Christmas Eve. A lighted candle is placed upon every grave in the old, walled-in cemetery. The same event occurs in Oberammergau, with the exception that each family substitutes a lighted Christmas tree on the graves of their dear departed. What is the meaning behind this custom? It is the German's way of honoring his dead, the candles symbolizing the rebirth of a new life.

Oberammergau . . . Berchtesgaden . . . Mittenwald . . . Garmisch . . . these are but a few enchanting stops among a virtual wonderland of Christmas holiday excursions awaiting the American serviceman. ■■

Scene from the Oberammergau Passion Play
—After interview with Jesus, Pilate says: "I can see no harm in this man"

TAKE TIME TO LIGHT THE FUSE!

By Rick Krepela

DID you ever lose a fortune—say a couple of hundred thousand dollars—just because you decided to quit when you were discouraged? It probably hasn't happened to many of us; or at least if it did we were spared the agony of knowing about it. The truth is, though, we never know what success we might have attained if only we had kept trying.

The language is full of clichés to make the point. One goes; "If at first you don't succeed, try, try again." How many times have we given up on a task because it "was a waste of time" or "hopeless"?

We are probably lucky that we turned back without ever realizing how close to success we were. Once in a while a man does learn what

Dexter was his name. He was a wiry prospector who had made a lucky "strike" or two in the mining camps of the 1870s. He was looking for a "big" strike—something to put himself on a par with the silver barons of the region. A promising claim was offered for sale so Dexter invested. It was hard cash—sixteen thousand dollars of it—that he tossed on the barrel head to buy an undeveloped claim called the Robert E. Lee mine.

At first it seemed like money well spent. On every knoll, in every hillside for miles around men were finding silver. A turn of a shovel was all that was needed to expose a new vein of ore! Or so it seemed.

At the Dexter mine—amidst all the fabulous claims—only dirt came into the mountain. Finally the shaft was over a hundred feet deep but still no silver was found.

News of other, productive mines in the region only made Dexter more discouraged. Five, ten, then almost fifteen thousand dollars went into the "worthless hole in the ground." He was determined not to lose the rest of his small fortune.

SOON it was known that the Robert E. Lee mine was up for sale. None of Dexter's friends could stop him from placing the mine on the block. With so much ore in the region surely a vein crossed the Robert E. Lee someplace?

Dexter failed to see it that way. He was very nearly broke; certainly discouraged. When a syndicate offered him thirty thousand dollars there was no haggling over the price. In fact, Dexter boasted that he "got my purchase price and almost what I put into that hole."

Before the sale was final he went to the shaft and told his men to stop work. "No sense my paying you to dig for a new owner," he told them.

At the end of the tunnel the men had just finished placing black powder charges into the rock. The fuses were all set to ignite!

"Can we touch off this last blast?" asked the foreman.

Dexter was furious. "Absolutely not. Not one more penny goes into this hole."

When the sale was completed the first thing the new owners did was to touch off the charge left behind by Dexter. The dust settled showing exposed veins of solid silver tracing through the rock.

Colorado mining records tell the story. The new owners took out $118,000 worth of silver in the first twenty-four hours.

While the Robert E. Lee mine became one of Colorado's richest producers Dexter had to live with the knowledge that his decision to quit had cost him a fortune. Perhaps we are lucky when most of us never know how "close we were" when we decide to turn back from a project.

But how foolish to quit after most of the work is done. It is never at the start of a task that we want to call it quits. Only after much work —perhaps most of it—does discouragement set in. But by then the "charges are set."

At least take the time to light the fuse.

■ ■

"They're okay, Lady. I was known in the carnival as 'Watt the Electric Man.'"

47

Truth in a Test Tube

By Lawrence P. Fitzgerald

DOES science know and religion guess? In some circles, this question would get an unqualified yes. For to some persons in our modern era, science commands uncritical admiration. To say that something is "scientific" is to pay it the supreme compliment.

But there are others who would reverse the sentence. They would say, Religion knows and science only guesses. Undoubtedly this is nearer to truth. But why say either? Why not say, Science knows some things; religion knows some things.

ence will cause you to lose your faith," she said. But he did not let this deter him. And now he says:

Today, I am happy to say, after many years of study and work in the field of science, my faith in God, rather than being shaken, has become much stronger and acquired a firmer foundation than heretofore . . . A deeper and firmer belief in God can be the only result of a better insight into truth . . .

(From *The Evidences of God* by John C. Monsma. Putnam. 1958. $3.75. This and other quotations from this important book used by permission.)

his rantings he denounced scientists and the textbooks in high school which sought to explain in scientific terms the origin of the universe. The Sunday school teachers followed his pattern and I was all confused. As a result, when I got to college and studied Biology, Zoology, Physics and learned how the world was formed, I lost my faith. I said, "If it is this way, the Bible cannot be true."

Do you blame Jack? Or do you blame Jack's teachers? Suppose Jack had had as his minister a man like Costen J. Harrell, who writes in a recent book, *I Believe in God* (Abingdon. 1958. $1.25):

There is no conflict between genuine science and true religion. Irreligious science and unreasonable religion are in continual disagreement. Our minds and tempers are steadied when we remember that all truth is God's truth, and that he does not contradict himself. The Lord of Nature is also the Lord of our souls.

What Is Science?

To understand the right relation between science and religion we need to have an accurate definition of science. *Science is the observation and classification of natural phenomena.* Its chief purpose is to formulate the general laws that operate in the natural world. Its chief methods are induction and hypothesis.

The Executive Director of Hormel Institution, Walter Oscar Lundberg, gives us the three elements of *the scientific method:*

1. The scientist observes and records selected natural phenomena.
2. He combines his observations with those provided by other scientists and draws conclusions and formulates working hypotheses.

3. If he wishes to test or validate his conclusions, he conducts additional and new observations, and determines if these agree with his predictions.

In short, the scientific method is founded on *orderliness* and *predictability* in natural phenomena.

Dr. Lundberg points out that this "orderliness and predictability" constitute a revelation of God in Nature. God is the author of this order and has given us a universe of dependable law. Without order and predictability and without God, the universe would be "a meaningless contradiction."

Science differs from religion in that science deals with the "how" whereas religion deals with the "why." Religion has been defined as "the life of God in the soul of man." Science can analyze and predict reactions in the 102 extremely diversified chemical elements. It can measure the amount of iron, salt, magnesium, sodium, phosphorous, sugar, and fat in a man; but it cannot test a man's love for his daughter. It cannot measure out a pound of right or a peck of wrong.

Yes, there is truth in a test tube; but the mistake sometimes made is to believe that all the truth is in the test tube. C. S. Lewis in his little book on *Miracles* (Association Press. 1958. 50 cents) well says:

The reason they find them intolerable (miracles) is that they start by taking Nature to be the whole of reality.

49

Now there is truth in Nature but to take Nature to be the whole of reality is a misconception of the first magnitude.

Our Debt to Science

Without doubt modern man owes a great debt to science. It would be impossible even to name all the many contributions of science to our way of life. But just to list a few very obvious ones:

Science has taught us to think honestly and objectively, not to be afraid of truth. It blasts superstition.

Science has given us a better understanding of our world. It has uncovered many of the secrets and wonders of the universe. One could wax poetic about the vastness of our universe—the sun's mass 330,000 times the 6,600 billion tons of the earth. And a billion suns in our galaxy larger than our sun. The universe contains 100,000 galaxies similar to ours. Then we could come from the bigness down to the atom. Science has split the atom and opened the door to unlimited power for the making of a better world.

Science has prolonged life. It is said our children will live 100 years; and our grandchildren will live 150 years.

Science has decreased suffering in the conquering of sickness and disease.

Science has given us modern gadgets which make life easier and more interesting; e.g., motor cars, jet planes, washing machines, radios, television. Science has made our world a great neighborhood.

One of the scientists who opened the way to the inside of the atom, Max Planck, says something with which most thinking Christians would agree:

Religion and Natural Science are fighting a joint battle in an incessant, never-relaxing crusade against skepticism, against dogmatism, and against superstition; and the rallying cry in this crusade has always been, and always will be: On to God!

The Inadequacy of Science

We have already suggested that some persons make the error of "taking Nature to be the whole of reality." Man is body; but man is also soul. There is a natural universe, but there is also a spiritual universe.

There is truth in a test tube; but not all the truth is in the test tube. There is also truth in a book—the Bible. There is truth in experience.

Now the Bible is not a scientific textbook; but nonetheless it is an inspired book. Through it God got his message to mankind. Behind its poetry and imagery and history and narrative is the great truth that ours is a spiritual universe. God is the Creator and Sustainer of his creation. In the sixty-six books of the Bible this mighty truth unfolds: Man, created in the image of God, sinned and fell away. God sought through the years to bring man back. In good time, he sent his only Son as Savior of the world to reveal God to men and to die upon the cross. Men through Christ would find the way to redemption, would learn how to gain abundant life here and hereafter.

These truths come not through science but through revelation and through experience. Indeed, it is essential that we discover and apply moral and spiritual truths for if we do not, through science we may unleash upon ourselves a power which will bring physical annihilation.

Testimony of Christian Scientists

In the significant book, *The Evidences of God in an Expanding Universe* edited by John Clover Monsma (Putnam. 1958. $3.75), forty American scientists declare their affirmative views on religion. These are outstanding scientists representing all branches of the physical and biological sciences from mathematics and astronomy to chemistry and nuclear physics. Hear what a few of these men say.

Irving Wm. Knobloch, Professor of Natural Sciences at Michigan State University, says:

But I believe in God. I believe in Him because I do not think that mere chance could account for the emergency of the first electrons, or the first atoms, or for the first seed, or for the first brain. I believe in God because to me His Divine existence is the only logical explanation for things as they are.

Edward Luther Kessel of the California Academy of Sciences, says:

To study science with an open mind will bring one to the necessity of a First Cause, whom we call God.

Russell Lowell Mixter, of the Illinois Academy of Science, points out:

There are probably a million species of animals on this earth . . . Of plants one could find at least two hundred thousand species . . . Order in such an array? There is order everywhere! . . . Logic compels us to assume that a Divine mind has conceived, planned and executed the variations and similarities here discussed . . .

When one reads in the Bible that God created man, animals, and plants, he can readily believe it, for what he has seen in Nature is in harmony with that belief. The Bible is not a textbook of science. But it does furnish the foundational principles of science.

Karl Heim in his recent volume *Christian Faith and Natural Science* phrased it thus:

The marvelous constitution of the world's structure not only *permits* the influence of an intellectual Creator, but *invites* such an inference.

Finally, Professor Edwin Conklin, biologist at Princeton University, has often said:

The probability of life originating from accident is comparable to the probability of the Unabridged Dictionary resulting from an explosion in a printing shop.

■■

AMONG OUR WRITERS

CAPT *Paul K. McAfee,* who wrote the fascinating story about a Korean Christmas with our armed forces ("The Three Strangers," page 5) is a chaplain now serving at Fort Rucker, Alabama . . . *Agnes Behling* ("In the Footsteps of Albert Schweitzer," page 10) has written several interesting and informative articles about outstanding personalities for THE LINK. Dr. Mellon has done a significant piece of work in his hospital in Haiti, which is modeled on Dr. Schweitzer's in Lambarene, Africa . . . *Rip Lynnfield* ("Christmas in the Bavarian Tyrol,' page 42) points up some of the experiences servicemen who are located in Germany may have during the Christmas holidays . . . We challenge you to check your knowledge of the biblical story of Christmas ("Christmas Quiz." page 19) by Vincent Edwards.

The trouble with some folks who give until it hurts is that they're so sensitive to pain.—Cy N. Peace

they paint by mouth and foot

By Steve Libby

←◀

Erich Stegmann holds brush in mouth
and puts finishing touches on painting

N OT everyone can paint, but to most of us writing our name is second nature.

Just for the fun of it, pick up a pencil with your mouth, and try writing your own name with it. Or, take off your shoes, grip a pencil between the toes, and try to write *anything* discernible.

By so doing, you will have some idea of the accomplishments by a group of sincere artists. For these artists are inspiring evidence of what determination can achieve in spite of unbelievable handicaps. They are members of the Association of Mouth and Foot Painting Artists, with members around the world and with headquarters in Vaduz, Liechtenstein.

Some time ago an exhibition of the work by these astounding men and women was held in London. In twelve days, hundreds of art fanciers studied the work, and critics from Great Britain and the Continent expressed amazement at the remarkable ability of these handicapped people.

The Vereinigung der Mund-und Fuse-malenden Kunstler cooperates with publishers in various countries to promote the art of mouth and foot-painting and assists the artists by creating a market for their work through the sale of greeting cards, calendars and picture prints which are reproduced from the paintings of the artists. It is in no way a charitable organization.

Members of this international group are not members because they have no use of their hands but, rather, because they are artists. The

52

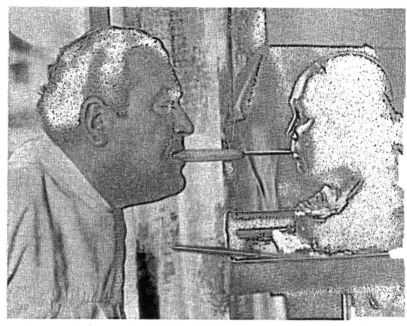

Stegmann is also a sculptor. With chisel in mouth he finishes a work of art

mouth
painting

London,
of art
k, and
and the
ment at
f these

und-und
operates
 countries
uth and
e artists
eir work
g cards,
s which
aintings
way a

national
use they
ds but,
sts. The

prize qualifications for membership include a standard of work which can compete in a commercial market with artists who have no such handicap—and the *will* to do so.

It is by that standard that their work is criticized and approved prior to membership.

IN the London exhibition were seventeen artists represented by seventy-four paintings, including sixteen oils, woodcuts, drawings and lithographs by perhaps the most amazing of all the members, Mr. Erich Stegmann. For it was Stegmann who thirteen years ago decided that all artists who paint by foot or mouth should work together and at that time founded the Association of which he is president and chairman. .

Paralyzed by poliomyelitis at the age of three, he learned to paint with his mouth and, by the time he was twenty, his work was being exhibited in several countries. Despite his handicap, he was a star pupil of the Academy at Munich and became a prolific painter in oils and a master of watercolor technique. He draws with pen and pencil and does lithographs. His linocuts with an engraver's tool in his mouth are brilliant, and his sculptures have won him international fame.

The formation of the Association was based on his premise that artists like himself could find it easier to market their work as a

53

group, and, freed from financial worry, they could then devote themselves to their art. He sought out two or three similarly handicapped artists, and visited them personally. The Association, with its headquarters in Liechtenstein, was finally established in February, 1956.

The next step was to arrange for the publication of reproductions of the members' work and to hold exhibitions. Publishers in fourteen countries now reproduce the pictures, and exhibitions have been held in seven nations.

THE London exhibition, one of the largest, displayed the work of a fairly representative group of members. Among the artists whose work was seen, the six which follow typify the entire membership.

Miss Phyllis Northcott, the middle-aged daughter of a British naval officer, lives in Devonshire. Some years ago she was seriously injured in a highway accident and has been since confined to her bed. As she cannot go out-of-doors, much of her work is copying. But with her mouth she paints the scene from her bedroom window and other Devon scenes.

Mr. A. Hext, another Briton from Ashburton, was born without arms

land, was an R.A.F. soldier before contracting polio. Having been interested in painting and drawing since school days, he employed occupational therapy to help him paint again and to develop his art. The R.A.F. Benevolent Fund gave him an opportunity to take lessons, and his success has been such that he has since married and is the father of a three-year-old son.

Miss Christine Perrott, only eighteen, contracted polio four years ago and has been in an iron lung ever since. She is allowed out of her life-giving contraption only three hours each day at her "residence," the Alexandra Hospital for Children at Luton, England. The Association presented her with a scholarship and she studies, painting for hours on end with her mouth. She copied a

Marie Louise Towae, twenty-three, native of France, paints with foot

portrait of the Queen, received a letter of encouragement. And she embroiders, writes poems and has started a Sunday school at the hospital.

From continental Europe—in addition to the Association's founder, Mr. Stegmann—were several representative paintings. Among them was the work of Mrs. Corry F. Riet, whose arms and legs are maimed. Her sensitive personality manifests itself in her delicate sea and landscapes. An orphan since early youth, she never knew the comfort of parental love or a happy home. But her art has given her material security as well as a full and satisfying life.

Miss Marie Louise Towae, born without arms in 1933, went to an elementary school and a high school for girls prior to an interruption by illness. Then Miss Towae dedicated herself to her painting and drawing. During her first year of training she won a competition, and her tutorship from Marthe Kiel and Robert Kuven has made her still-life pictures and landscapes, painted with her feet, in considerable demand.

Today there are more than twenty artists in the Association—and none of them pay membership fees or dues of any kind. Seven handicapped artists are today receiving scholarships from the Association, whose finances come from a small percentage of profits from publishers who purchase the work of members.

■■

Records, Records, Records! You'll find one in almost every sport. Here's a record made in a snowshoe marathon, held in 1945. Lloyd Evans of St. Hyacinthe, Canada, snowshoed his way to a new world's record. He did it in 59:23, knocking two seconds off the ten-mile mark. Some snowshoeing!

PHOTO CREDITS

Page 10, 12, 14 and 15, The Grant Foundation; page 31, United Voluntary Services; pages 43, 45, German Tourist Information Office; pages 52, 53, 54, Association of Mouth and Foot Painting Artists; page 60, U.S. Navy.

WORTH QUOTING: The secret of economy is to live as cheaply the first few days after payday as you lived the last few days before.—*Arkansas Baptist* . . .. Scene Stealer: A guy who puts up billboards.—Francis O. Walsh

THE HIGH LINE

By H. L. Reid

IT was the end of a perfect day. We had visited the little town of Bethlehem where our Savior was born. As I lay in my bed at the Imperial Hotel in Jerusalem, through the transom I could see the stars over the big wide glass doors leading to the porch. The sky was remarkably clear and I remembered only one place I'd been where the stars shone with such brilliance—the Allegheny Mountains of Virginia where I began my ministry several years ago.

As I thought of the events of the day I tried to picture the original Christmas scene—the rustle and the bustle of the Holy City; the long arduous journey of Mary and Joseph over the rough winding road that led to Bethlehem; the over-crowded inn and the occupants that night; the cave or stable which appears to be one of the most authentic remains today; the star that stood over the stable very high in the heavens!

For sailors in foreign ports this twentieth century there will be another memorable scene at Christmas time. High above the waters and stretched between two ships a "High Line" will transport the Navy chaplain from one ship to another. Equipped with a life jacket, he will be strapped securely in a small metal chair hanging from a pulley and swinging in the breeze. Santa in all his glory is not arrayed like one of these! There will be no red-nosed reindeer to expedite the trip. Men on the host ship will tug strenuously at a rope to insure the chaplain's safe arrival.

All hands turn out to make the operation a success. A lot of planning and hard work go into rigging what one ship calls their "high ball express." Men not engaged in the operation will be on deck with their cameras—and comments—as they welcome the chaplain aboard. In spite of numb and bleeding hands of the officers and enlisted men who rig it, the High Line is a fellowship that lifts our eyes to the higher things of life. Ever since the first cries were heard from the manger in Bethlehem nearly two thousand years ago, millions of persons have been gazing upward to the High Line of life. The eyes of the *wise men;* the eyes of little children before a glittering Christmas tree; the eyes of homeless refugees; the eyes of those who bear the mark of pain; the eyes of the aged and broken-hearted; the eyes of the bruised and the captives; the eyes of the persecuted; the eyes of the lonely and the eyes of the men at sea! ■ ■

TRACTION

By Paul E. Carson

THE other day a veteran said to me, "Chaplain, when you have lost your confidence and become despondent, *you have lost your traction on the terrestrial ball.*"

He grinned a little at the way he expressed it, yet what he said has significance for us all.

Lack of confidence has a tendency to make you despondent. And when you are despondent you lack the traction, the power to accomplish things. Traction is defined as "the act of drawing or pulling; the adhesive friction of a body, as of a wheel on a rail."

Anyone who has watched a great locomotive knows what a tremendous traction is necessary to put the train in motion. If the tracks are wet or oily, they are slippery and the wheels merely spin around.

But provision has been made for just such an event. The engineer presses a lever and some sand drops on the rails. This gives the wheels the necessary traction, the sparks begin to fly, and the train begins to move.

How can you regain your traction, your power to influence others and attract them to the better things of life? By *doing something about it,* like the engineer and the sand.

"But, Chaplain," you object, "that is not as simple as it sounds."

AND you are right. However, you must do something. Try doing things that are positive, and practical. Remember, our Lord taught us to pray and to ask God to help us even though he already knows our needs.

Like the young soldier who came to me with his problem.

"Chaplain," he said, "I am in trouble and I have to go AWOL to straighten it out."

He told me his story and we talked it over so that we had a complete picture of what was involved. Then, by his own decision, he did not go AWOL. This would simply have made his problem greater.

There are times when the traction may be getting a little weak, and you need something to help the wheels take hold. Having someone listen to you as you unburden yourself of your anxiety may be all that is necessary.

Then the sparks will begin to fly. You will have a new confidence in yourself and in other people. Your new traction will give you power you may not have realized was possible, and you will have a peace in your heart.

And remember, there is One who is *always* ready to listen when you are willing to place your confidence in Him. ■ ■

57

Let Us Pray

Loving Father, as we go on our happy ways, suddenly we are beset with darkness, doubt, fear, anxiety. We know not how to face these anxious moments of life as we ought. But thou hast said in thy Word that we shall not suffer temptation beyond our strength to endure; so we pray now for this strength, for thy presence, for the presence of thy Holy Spirit to meet this hour.

Teach us, O God, how to integrate these experiences into our lives so we may be stronger, so we may have more patience, more understanding, more kindness toward others. We see how weak we all are, how unable to cope with the trials and temptations of life without thy help. So may we trust in thee. Give us the steadfastness and faithfulness to persevere in spite of the stumbling blocks set along our way.

Holy Father, we are thy children and we ask thee to illuminate our path, make firm our step, and walk with us along the rough places as well as the smooth. Through Jesus Christ, our Lord. *Amen.*

Quicken, O Lord, we beseech thee, all the members of thy church that they may be alive to the opportunities and responsibilities of these times. Save us from complacency and from fear of new ways; inspire our minds with a vision of a world won for thee, and stir our wills to pray and to work until thy will is done on earth as it is in heaven; for Jesus' sake. *Amen.*

O most gracious and loving Father, we would be like a tree planted by streams of water . . . standing steadfast . . . bringing forth fruit . . . bending with the wind but not becoming uprooted. We confess that too often we have failed thee; we have sinned, we have missed the mark, we have gone astray.

What we need, O Father, and we pray for it, is thy forgiveness and thy healing and the strength of thy abiding presence. Thou art our creator. Now re-create us strong and rocklike. Purify our diseased souls. O thou Great Physician, it is thy healing we need. Thou art the physician of the souls of men. Come into our hearts. Strengthen us in body, in mind, in spirit. Give us the peace of God in the midst of the tumult. In spite of the strong will to sin in us all, make our wills thine and help us to pray: Not my will but thine be done. Through Jesus Christ, our Lord. *Amen.*

Heavenly Father, our divine companion, we thank thee for the wonderful, inspiring companionship of friends and loved ones. Many of our loved ones are far from us today. Watch over them, protect them, keep them close to us by bonds of love and prayer. Make us worthy of their great love. For the many friendly folk around us we give thee thanks. Make us appreciative of this rich brotherhood. And most of all, may we walk and talk with thee, our divine companion. Through Jesus Christ. *Amen.*

58

The Link
Satellite

We view developments in the world of religion

More on World Refugee Year

World Refugee Year is now in full progress. The World Council of Churches has called upon its members in fifty-two countries to pray and act in behalf of displaced persons. Says the Council: "We are convinced that in our day and generation our greatest human tragedy is that of the refugee—homeless people all around the world."

There are an estimated 45,000,000 refugees in the world today, including 27,575,000 in Asia, another 18,015,000 in Europe and 170,000 in Africa.

Those wishing to inform their groups on the refugee problem may order from the World Council of Churches, 17, Route de Malagnou, Geneva, Switzerland: Picture sheets for display on bulletin boards; glossy prints of pictures; and documentary films. Four films are available: *Like Paradise, The Long Stride, Each Year in May,* and the newest, *Old Believers.*

New Library for Japan

The International Christian University in Japan is building a $425,-000 library on its campus in Mitaka-shi, Tokyo. Work started last summer. It will be a three-story building with a total of 27,284 square feet of floor space and will shelve more than 157,000 volumes. Funds for the building are being raised by The Japan International Christian University Foundation, Inc., 44 E. 23rd St., New York 10, N.Y.

Air Force Choir Winners

Congratulations to the Chapel Choir of Bartow Air Force Base, Florida, which won first place in the fourth annual U.S. Air Force Chapel Choir Contest. Second place went to the Chapel Choir of Ernest Harmon Air Force Base, a SAC base in Newfoundland. Dreux Air Base, France, USAF in Europe, received third place. Honorable mention was given to the choir of Walker Air Force Base, New Mexico.

59

CDR Cagle, Exec. Off. of *Intrepid*, conducts morning devotions in ship's hobby shop. Lay leaders are rendering great service

International Prayer

Mrs. Joy de Leon, R.N., of Madison, Wisconsin, now serving as a nurse in the Methodist Church's *Sanatoria Palmore* in Chihuahua, Mexico, has composed an international prayer which is attracting wide attention. The prayer:

"God grant that I may have the Latin love of beauty, the African sense of the ridiculous, the Indian mysticism, the Jewish faith, the American know-how, the European know-why, the Greek moderation, and the Christian love. Amen."

Go to Church and Get a Divorce

An East German court has ruled that active participation in church life constitutes "strong grounds for divorce," reports the Ecumenical Press from Bolivia. In awarding a divorce the court said that "progressive-thinking people in our state of workers and farmers cannot be expected to remain tied to a marriage partner who leans more and more towards the church." The case involved a woman who led "a good married life at first," but lately she attends services on Sunday and takes part in other church activities "at least twice a week." In so doing the defendant "created an estrangement between herself and her husband which constitutes sufficient grounds for divorce."

New Youth Secretary

The Rev. Roderick S. French, a minister of the Protestant Episcopal Church, has been appointed associate secretary in the Youth Department of the World Council of Churches. He took up his work in Geneva on September 1. Mr. French is twenty-eight and former curate of the Church of the Ascension in New York City.

Science and Religion

The title of this section of THE LINK is also the name of a bulletin issued by The Committee on Religion and Science, 11 W. 42nd St., New York 36, N.Y. *The Satellite* contains digests of magazine articles, news items, book reviews, poetry, hymns, sermons and quotes. Ministers, scientists, and others in the field of leadership who might wish to use scientific and religious materials in combating materialism may become members of this committee and receive free literature.

Heart-Lung Machine

Dr. Robert E. Gross of Children's Hospital, Boston, Mass. has perfected a heart-lung machine, first announced in 1957, which has been used in more than 250 operations on the heart and the nearby great blood vessels. "One of the great difficulties in the country today," says Dr. Gross, "is acquiring blood for medical and surgical use." By the use of the machine which he and his associates have perfected, two operations may be performed in succession on persons with the same blood type. Dr. Gross comments: "Recently we started one operation at 8 o'clock in the morning. It was completed by 10:30. We did the second case without re-priming the machine, completed it and went to lunch at 12:30 —a double-header, you might say." To recover the blood left in the machine after an operation for later use, it is drained off into plastic bags. "On many occasions," Dr. Gross reported, "we have recovered the remaining blood and re-employed it within the next few days, if necessary."

Now If We'll Just Read Them

The American Bible Society during 1958 distributed over the world 16,629,496 volumes of the Scriptures. Distribution in the United States reached a total of 9,188,987 volumes.

I am the door: by me if any man enter in, he shall be saved, and shall go in and out, and find pasture.   JOHN 10:9

Our Bible verse points up the truth that Jesus is the door to salvation and to freedom. Man in *bondage to sin* finds his true freedom as he puts himself in the hands of Jesus Christ. He then "goes in and out and finds pasture." All this is made possible through the incarnation. "The word became flesh and dwelt among us." In the Babe of Bethlehem, the Jesus of Galilee, and the Christ of Calvary, we have victory!

The Link Calendar

DECEMBER is an important month for Christians for during this month comes Christmas, the festival celebrating the birth of our Lord. The traditional date is December 25, although the evidence of the New Testament gives weight to the belief Jesus was born in the Springtime. However, the *time* is not most important; what is important is that we honor the incarnation, the reality that God came down into time in the person of Jesus, the Son.

Advent has already begun as the month opens. It begins on the Sunday nearest St. Andrew's Day, November 30, and lasts the four weeks preceding Christmas. But make much of the preparation for Christmas. Note the article "Get Ready for Christmas" (page 16).

Dec. 1-31: Eleventh International Photography Exhibit, Bordeaux, France.

Dec. 2: Pan-American Health Day.

Dec. 5-11: Six-Day Bike Race, Copenhagen, Denmark.

Dec. 6: St. Nicholas Day in some countries—Holland, Belgium, and parts of Germany. Not a bad idea, have Santa Claus come on the sixth and reserve December 25 for the worship of Christ.

Dec. 10: Award Nobel Prizes—Oslo, Norway and Stockholm, Sweden.

Dec. 13: Universal Bible Sunday.

Dec. 15: Bill of Rights Day. On this day in 1791 the Bill of Rights was ratified. December is also the eleventh anniversary of the adoption of the Universal Declaration of Human Rights (adopted December, 1948).

Dec. 15-Jan. 6: Pageant of Peace, Washington, D.C.

Dec. 17: Anniversary of Powered Flight. The first successful airplane flight made by the Wright brothers, Kitty Hawk, N.C., Dec. 17, 1903.

Dec. 20: Christmas Sunday.

Dec. 22: Winter begins at 9:35 A.M.

Dec. 24: Christmas Eve. Many churches have a Christmas Eve Worship Service, honoring the birthday of Christ, our Savior.

Dec. 25: Christmas Day falls on Friday this year.

Dec. 26-30: International Ice Hockey Championship, Davos, Switzerland.

Dec. 29-Jan. 1: Mid-Winter Sports Carnival, New Orleans, La.

Dec. 31: New Year's Eve. Many churches have a Watch Night Service and pray the old year out and the new year in.

Helps for Lay Leaders

THE two great festivals of the Christian church are Christmas and Easter. The first of these we celebrates this month—December. It should be a time of rejoicing, if we dig down and discover the real meaning of Christmas—that Christ is born, that Christ is found, that Christ is to be shared!

The four study articles this month should help us achieve these objectives. And as we look forward to the new year, let us see that our faith is founded upon the truth as we study "Truth in a Test Tube."

1. Get Ready for Christmas (see page 16)

The Main Idea: For many, getting ready for Christmas means merely buying all their gifts; but there is a need also for getting ready in the heart, making room for Christ, discovering the deeper meaning of Christmas.

Bible Material: Luke 2:1-20.

Discussion Questions: What is the meaning of Advent? Why should we get ready for Christmas? How get ready for Christmas?

Hymns: "We Three Kings of Orient Are"; "As With Gladness Men of Old"; "It Came Upon a Midnight Clear."

2. A Doctor Writes a Book (see page 28)

The Main Idea: Dr. Luke of New Testament times wrote one of the most beautiful Gospels to show how Christ died for everyone, not just Israel alone. Just as God guided the doctor, Luke, he is still guiding the hand of those in the medical profession.

Bible Material: Luke 1:1-4, 26-38.

Discussion Questions: Who was Luke? Why did he want to write a Gospel? What are the main features of his Gospel? How does it differ from the other Gospels? What about the faith of doctors and nurses today?

Hymns: "The First Noel"; "Joy to the World"; "Hark, the Herald Angels Sing."

3. Why My Mother Disliked Christmas? (see page 40)

The Main Idea: Many pagan customs have grown up around Christmas which make some people dislike it. We should rescue Christmas and bring it back to its central emphasis—the birth of Jesus Christ, the Son of God, and our Savior.

Bible Material: Matthew 2:1-12.

Discussion Questions: What elements about Christmas do you dislike? Like? What pagan elements are intermingled with the Christmas celebration? How can we make Christmas truly Christian? How can you make the Christmas spirit last the year around?

Hymns: "Silent Night, Holy Night"; "O Little Town of Bethlehem"; "O Come All Ye Faithful."

4. Truth in a Test Tube (see page 48)

The Main Idea: Science commands great respect and some persons think that "the test tube" is the only way to knowledge. However, there is truth in the Book and in experience as well as in science. Actually, there is no real conflict between true science and true religion, for God is not only the creator of the world who established its laws; but he is the author of our religious yearnings, too.

Bible Material: 1 Corinthians 2.

Discussion Questions: What is science? What is religion? What is the relation of scientific truth and religious insight? How has science helped religion? How does religion help science? What is the attitude of scientists toward religion?

Hymns: "Lead Kindly Light"; "Lead On, O King Eternal"; "Take My Life, and Let It Be."

Books Are Friendly Things

The Bible Speaks to Daily Needs by George Harkness (Abingdon Press, 1959, $1.50).

An excellent little devotional guide written by the gifted writer and penetrating thinker who is professor of applied theology at Garrett Biblical Institute. What do you do in time of doubt, trouble, temptation, when you are lonely, when God seems far away, etc., etc. G. H. guides you to the Bible and to prayer and asks some soul-searching questions. There are eighty-six devotionals.

I Found God in Soviet Russia by John Noble and Glenn D. Everett (St. Martin's Press, 1959, $2.95).

This is a poorly written book, much too long and repetitious, but it does show two things: (1) the difficulties of living in a police state; and (2) that a praying man can find God no matter how trying the difficulties are.

Noble was swallowed up in the Russian zone of Germany shortly after V-E Day, in 1945, and spent ten years in Soviet prisons. For many months, he was kept in the dark as to why he was arrested; he existed on a bread diet, two ounces daily; he saw only fifteen of 21,000 prisoners liberated; and on every hand he witnessed cruelty, immorality, indecency. Yet through prayer he was saved and "found God." The old question of why God says yes to one and no to another is not answered—perhaps cannot be; but at any rate here is one man who found God in the desperate tragedy of atheism and brutality.

God in My Life by Lloyd C. Wicke (Abingdon, 1959, $1.00). -

"Look about you and within and discern His power and His divinity. It is clearly evident." Paraphrasing Paul's statement in Romans 1:20, Lloyd C. Wicke sets the scene for the exploration into the inner life of a Christian and then examines some ways in which we may more clearly sense the divine power of God. With spiritual insight, the author explores such personal concerns as the meaning of existence, the significance of faith, prayer, the Bible, the church, one's vocation, and the like.

Sound Off! _

Sound Off! (*continued from page 4*)

From a Member of EMCU

It was a joy and inspiration for me to read the article concerning "Marines Who Tell the Story of Christ." . . . Servicemen have a dynamic potential to reach others for Christ . . . They get to places that missionaries have not had the privilege of going . . . Reaching others for Christ should begin right where we are, in the barracks, on ships, on the shores, and in the homes of military personnel . . .

Perhaps your magazine could be a means of supplying service personnel with information concerning places to make contact with other Christians in the service, and a source of information as to places to get together for Bible study, prayer, and Christian fellowship.

> Alfred W. Prince, SFC, USA,
> Enlisted Men's Christian Union,
> Ft. Windfield Scott, Calif.

(*Specific dates would be hard to give, for we publish so far in advance; but we're glad to mention places where men meet for Bible study, prayer, and Christian fellowship and regular meeting dates. However, this perhaps may best be done through personal contact. L.P.F.*)

From the Reformed Church

Dear Editor:

On behalf of the Chaplain's Commission of the Reformed Church in America, I am happy to commend you for the excellent magazine THE LINK. We feel that you are producing a magazine for our servicemen which is readable, informational, and inspirational.

> John H. Muller, Sect.
> Chaplain's Commission, RCA,
> Chicago, Ill.

Still Reads the Link

I have been out of the Air Force since December 5, 1958 and am doing quite well as a civilian. I really enjoyed reading THE LINK while working for the chaplains in the service. I think that it is the best magazine out when it comes to reading enjoyment. Please let me know what it costs for a yearly subscription.

> John B. Estlack,
> Thomas Nelson & Sons,
> Camden, N.J.

65

At Ease!

POST EXCHANGE

DRESS GLOVES
DRESS GLOVES
DRESS GLOVES

ALVIN HALE

A sermon on the benevolence of the Lord didn't fall on deaf ears last Sunday in one church. As the collection plate was being passed, one little pre-school tyke reached in and took a handful of coins. As his shocked mother tried to get him to put the cash back, he cried out: "But it's my money! God gave it to me!"

Western Nebraska Observer

A mother in Boston is still telling about this little repartee between herself and her small son on the well-known night before Christmas. Becoming aware of an unusual silence in the youngster's room, she called out warily, "Johnny, what are you doing?"

"Nothing," came the disgusted answer. "With you and God and Santa Claus all watching, what *can* I do?"

Mother decided that ten-year-old Kathy should get something "practical" for Christmas. "Suppose we open a savings account for you?" mother suggested. Kathy was delighted.

"It's your account, darling," mother said as they arrived at the bank, "so you fill out the application."

Kathy was doing fine until she came to the space for "Name of your former bank." After a slight hesitation, she put down "piggy."

—American Weekly

Bob Campbell has preserved a typical weather report from a tourist-conscious resort in southern California: "Rain and heavy winds all yesterday and today. Continued fair tomorrow."

Bennett Cerf in *The Life of the Party*

The proud·father invited a professional opera singer to come to his house one night and listen to his daughter sing.

After his daughter's performance, the beaming parent turned to the great vocalist and asked, "How did you like it? What do you think of her execution?"

"I think," replied the opera singer, "I'd be in favor of it."

—Pageant

66

Lightning Source UK Ltd.
Milton Keynes UK
UKHW010607120219
337137UK00007B/1530/P